Buddy Moon

City of Grove Series

Lisa & Tom

Rhonda K. Boehm

CHAPTER 1

"Ooh, now here's something nice for you to take along," Lisa Collins said as she picked up a sexy red baby doll nightgown and showed it to her best friend. They were in Olive's bedroom getting ready for the big trip.

"Hmmm, I like that one too," Olive said. "If I put any more in my suitcase, I won't be able to close it," she laughed.

Lisa giggled. "This is little. Just squish it right here in the corner."

And she did so.

Olive smiled and giggled too.

"Olive!" Lisa gushed. "I can't believe you're taking all of us along on your honeymoon. It's going to cost a mint!"

"Oh, don't worry about it," Olive said, waving her hand in dismissal. "Mason and I talked about it and want you guys to come along. It's called a buddy moon. Three couples join the bride and groom on their honeymoon. Don't worry, Lisa. There will be so many public displays of affection, you know, PDA, between Mason and me that you won't be able to stand it."

"Well, I appreciate it. And I'm sure the others do too."

"My dad is paying for it. He said he doesn't mind. He said it was his wedding present to us."

Olive's dad was a VP for an oil company, and money seemed no object. "Maui is such a romantic place for a wedding," Lisa raved. "Then we'll tour the Hawaiian Islands as a group. That is still just awesome! For a few days, after the wedding, we'll be on our own, but mostly we'll go as a group everywhere. And I like that."

But in this case, none of the attendees were really couples. The six attendees had not even met each other yet. Lisa and Tom—the best man—were supposed to be a couple, but she hadn't met him yet.

"I'm so excited," Olive gushed suddenly.

Lisa smiled. "I hope to be as happy as you are one day. But with what happened… I don't know…"

"That was so long ago, Lisa. Things are different now. I know that happened in the past, but now, maybe you can be contented." Olive dipped her chin and looked at Lisa. "You'll like Tom. He's Mason's best friend from college."

"Olive…" Lisa started.

"No, you *will* like him. He's funny and charismatic. And he's cute."

"Don't let Mason hear you say that," Lisa chuckled.

"Oh, I've already told Mason. He doesn't care. He trusts me. Besides, you're the maid of honor and he's the best man. Of course you have to get together," Olive laughed.

"Does he know this?" Lisa asked, cringing.

"Mason was supposed to tell him."

"Oh, Olive," Lisa groaned. "I don't know. What if I can't get along with Tom? What if what happened in high school prevents that?"

"Lisa, it's been eight years. You have to jump back into life at some point and *not* let that jerk win."

"I went to art school," Lisa mumbled. "I moved on."

"With everything but men." Olive looked pointedly at Lisa. "When was the last time you had a date?"

"I don't remember. It's been a while." Lisa made a face. "I don't want to talk about it anymore."

"Okay, but I'm matching you up with Tom."

Lisa hoped he had a great personality. According to Olive, he did, but Olive was always trying to play matchmaker.

Lisa sighed heavily. The traffic was awful.

"Yes, Lisa. We'll get there on time," Sophia spoke up, as if reading Lisa's thoughts.

"I just don't want to miss the plane," Lisa moaned, nervously running her hand through her hair until she realized how long it had taken to get it styled before they left for the trip, then she stopped before she messed it up. It always took hours for her hair to get done. This time, she had gotten it styled and cut just right before leaving for the trip.

"We've got plenty of time," Emma chimed in.

"She's right, you know," Alice confirmed, in the driver's seat. "We left early. When I drop you off, you can check your bags. You won't be late."

Lisa looked at her friends—Sophia, Emma, and Alice—from elementary school. They were going on the vacation of a lifetime. Too bad Alice couldn't join them. She was just driving them to the airport that morning but not going on the buddy moon. They would drive into Houston this afternoon from their little town of Grove, Texas.

Lisa hoped Olive was right about Tom. She recalled unbearable shyness that she had endured since her bad experience in high school. Would her inner demons ever let her rest and find someone nice?

"Okay, I'll relax," Lisa said. "I helped Olive pack yesterday. Then, I went home and packed my own suitcase. I was up very late last night." She was nervous and excited and just wanted to sleep now. She was also so tired from lack of sleep. There would be time to sleep on the plane, but she didn't want to miss anything. Maybe if she opened her eyes wider, she could stay awake, but they refused to stay open.

"That's better. Now, what did you pack for the wedding?" Sophia asked Emma.

As the others started discussing the wedding, Lisa relaxed and leaned back in her seat. Her eyelids grew heavy. They were going to a wedding in Hawaii—Olive and Mason's wedding. A buddy moon. Sophia and Emma were also bridesmaids in the wedding.

The car slowed down.

Lisa sat up. "Did I doze off?" she asked the group, incredulous.

"Yes, you were snoring loudly," Sophia snorted, laughing.

"I did not!"

Everyone else laughed. They pulled up to the side of the airport, piled out of the car, and grabbed their suitcases from the back of the SUV. Alice had borrowed her dad's Mercedes SUV so the three women could ride together. The guys pulled up behind them—Tom, Bill, and Noah with Jim driving. Then, the wedding couple, Olive and Mason, arrived.

Olive's dad dropped them off, parking his Cadillac behind the guys. Lisa considered the trip ahead and gazed at everyone.

Eight people, four couples who aren't really couples but going to Maui together, she thought.

"Lisa, this is Tom. Tom, Lisa," Olive introduced them.

Lisa was suddenly excited again. Tom locked eyes with her. His eyes were so baby-blue, they pierced her soul. He was drop-dead gorgeous in his six-foot-one frame. His button-down white shirt fit across his upper torso and muscular arms perfectly. The shirt was tucked into black jeans, hugging his trim waist. With that luscious black hair and a lock falling in his face, he had chiseled good looks. When she looked up, she found that he caught her checking him out.

He smiled.

She flushed and ducked her head, putting a blonde stray hair behind her ear. Would she ever change? Lisa wished she wasn't so shy.

She looked up again. He was still staring, and he flashed another dimpled smile that made her pulse thrum. Lisa smiled back.

"Look who's ogling you," Sophia whispered in Lisa's ear.

Lisa didn't mean to blush, but it came on too easily. The blush started at the roots of her hair and ran down to her toes. Whenever Tom looked her way, she turned bright red and her brain turned to mush. Words failed her. Tom was hot. His smoldering blue eyes kept looking her way. Lisa was speechless, and her face turned red. Her breathing escalated, and her heartbeat slammed against her chest like a cartoon character. She thought everyone must see it—must hear it. Lisa couldn't catch her breath. Sophia bumped Lisa's shoulder again.

Lisa breathed in and out.

Calm down. He's just looking my way. That's all. That's all? That's everything!

Lisa reached for her suitcase and handed it to the porter. The porter weighed her luggage. Just a pound under the limit.

"What a relief," she sighed.

"Did you pack rocks?" Tom asked in his deep male voice. Lisa jumped and looked Tom in the eye. When he smiled, dimples popped out in his checks. "It's okay. The weight's just right."

"Yeah, the rocks I packed were perfect." Lisa couldn't help herself. She ducked her head… again but looked back up at Tom. Her brain didn't work, but her smile did. Her mother always told her to smile when she was speechless around boys. Lisa smiled a lot.

Sophia bumped Lisa, who fell into Tom. "My rocks need to be weighed."

"Sophia!" Lisa exclaimed, scrambling to keep from falling. Quickly, Tom steadied her. The skin on her shoulders burned with excitement. An electric shock ran down her arms and to her toes. She breathed in deeply, smelling Tom's cologne—a cedar and woodsy spice and something else… his male scent. There was a magnetic attraction. Something pulled her to him. Chemistry?

Ahh, he smelled so good.

CHAPTER 2

*T*om Jeffreys smiled into Lisa's deep blue eyes. He just wanted to get her alone but not here, so he could talk to her.

She smiled back. *Awesome.* Her shoulder-length blonde hair was curled just right on her five-foot-six frame. Her blush was sexy, and his mouth went dry. Her pink sundress showed off her curves just right across her breast and fell loosely on her hips. The dress hit halfway up her thighs.

Tom had a reputation that he could schmooze anyone in conversation. Yet here he was… tongue-tied. Now that the gift of gab actually mattered, he couldn't think of a thing to say. He was nervous and excited about this trip and her.

Tom had been in a serious relationship last year, but it ended badly. Dating had become a series of one-night stands, casual no strings attached.

He thought about being with her for two weeks and began imaging her in a different light. He was the best man, and Lisa was the maid of honor. It was like they were already a couple. Now, he wondered would this shy beautiful blonde, who smelled like lilac and took his breath away, be the one? Or would the ghosts of his past stop this relationship before it even started?

"TJ!" Mason shouted and slapped Tom on the back so hard he almost lost his balance all the while holding on to Olive's waist with the other hand.

Only Mason called him TJ. Mason always shortened everyone's name. Mason just didn't know his own strength. Mason had been a star football player in college.

Tom reached out and grabbed Lisa again, but this time, she was ready. She was facing Mason and Olive, whereas Tom had his back to Mason, facing Lisa.

"Are you excited or what?" Tom turned and laughed at Mason.

"I am thrilled," Olive spoke up. Bill and Noah came up and set their luggage down.

The guys' luggage was smaller and lighter than the women's. The men were going to get their tuxes in Hawaii. They didn't have to pack those. The women had to pack their bridesmaid dresses. Carefully. They'd get steamed once they got there.

The wedding would be in the early part of the week, then the group would start touring the islands after that. They were staying there for two weeks. Olive's family would fly in tomorrow, but this group—the buddy moon group—would start today.

"Everyone checked in?" Mason boomed.

"Mason, not so loud," Olive whispered. "We're all here. Now that our luggage is checked in, let's get checked through security."

The group walked along, with Bill and Noah clowning around, Sophia and Emma egging them on. Mason and Olive led the group. Tom and Lisa lagged behind.

"What do you do for a living?" Tom asked Lisa as they strolled along the corridor of the airport.

"I'm a painter," Lisa answered, smiling to herself. "I'm working on getting a showing at a gallery. I'm in negotiations with Bella's Gallery downtown. I hope I don't jinx it by mentioning it." Lisa looked up at Tom, raising her eyebrows. "And you? What do you do?"

"I'm an architect for my dad's firm, Jefferys' and Sons. Not too far from Bella's Gallery. Bella's will be quite a nice showing. That's a great place."

"Well, I'm not there yet." Lisa pursed her lips, raising her eyebrows with a big sigh.

"I have no doubt you'll get that gig. I just barely finished the project I was working on before we left, but my brother will take it to the client and make any necessary changes while I am away." When she didn't reply, he continued,

"I'm worried there is a piece that will take longer than originally planned." Tom was trying to keep the conversation going as they headed to the gate to wait for their flight.

As they ambled through the airport, people were talking, kids were jumping, babies were crying, and announcements were broadcasted through the loudspeakers. Numerous people were standing at the kiosk to check-in electronically instead of standing in line. After the group checked in, they headed for the gate area to wait for their flight. Mason and Olive sat all lovey-dovey snuggled up together. Bill and Noah kept trying to get Sophia and Emma's attention as if they didn't have it already, and Tom and Lisa stood together, talking. The line to the check-in desk was long, but Olive had gotten them first-class tickets all together, so they were in the front of the line to board. Tom managed to maneuver and sit by Lisa—two seats on each side of the middle aisle. They were huge seats. First-class was the way to go.

CHAPTER 3

Lisa didn't like landings or takeoffs. She held onto the armrest with one hand and the e-reader with the other. She sat straight up in her seat. The butterflies were bumping into each other in her stomach.

Tom laid his hand on hers. Her heart raced the minute his hand touched hers. She shivered. Those butterflies turned into bumblebees buzzing around. She could feel the electricity from touching him. She looked over and tried to smile, but it turned into a grimace because she was still so terrified about flying. He smiled and crinkles formed at the corners of his eyes. She liked that. He probably laughed a lot too. And his dimples… what a combo. The group was flying out of Houston to Dallas.

"Don't crush your e-reader with that death grip you've got there," Tom joked.

Despite her tense muscles, Lisa laughed.

And they took off down the runway.

She took a big breath and relaxed a little bit. Tom looked at her concerned. Lisa shivered.

Her breathing was deep, and her chest rose and fell in rapid succession. She stared into his dark-blue eyes, and her heart melted. If he kept this up, she would soon be a puddle at his feet.

He leaned over and bumped his shoulder into hers as they held hands.

And the plane lifted into the air.

Lisa was too caught up in Tom's gaze to notice.

Tom smiled. "Looks like we're flying," he said, his voice low and gravely.

"Yes, we are," Lisa whispered, still breathing deeply.

They talked the entire time on the short flight from Houston to Dallas.

"Tell me what you do weekly," Tom inquired. "You told me you are an artist. Tell me about your daily routine."

"Such a tall order." Lisa smiled, breathing out and calming down some. "On Monday through Thursday, I either take a client or paint or sculpt my own work. When I take on a client, it usually takes several sittings to get the painting right. Depending on their schedules, they come back three times a week till that painting is just right. It usually takes three weeks, but it can go longer."

"What do you do on the weekends? Friday through Sunday?" Tom smirked. "Relax? Play? Goof off? Play golf? I got it! Work your fingers to the bone!"

Lisa laughed. "Well, sometimes, but what I really do is volunteer at the Children's Museum, giving lessons in painting on Fridays. Sometimes, we mix it up and do sculpture, calligraphy, ceramics, computer/graphic design." She thumped the top of her lip while she thought about what else they taught. "There are Christian or religious classes, graffiti, stained glass, mosaic, or tapestry," she laughed. "Sometimes we bring in specialists, and sometimes I teach it all!" Lisa could feel her eyes widen as she always got excited about her volunteer work.

Tom laughed.

"I had no idea how to do a few, like computer/graphic design and tapestry. I had to learn those mediums before I could teach them. There was a real-time crunch. The Children's Museum wanted to teach each of those, and I had to learn them. Fast," she said, smiling knowingly.

"Wow!" Tom chuckled. "You did all those at once?"

"Oh, no. Thank God!" Lisa giggled. "One at a time."

"Which do you like best?" Tom asked.

"That's hard to say. Painting mostly. Oil's more forgiving than other mediums," Lisa started, getting animated. "That means watercolor is dry and done after a day. Sometimes, after an hour, you can paint over it. But you can't change the basic color already on the page unlike in oil."

"Yeah, I took an oil painting class when I was in architecture school. Just for grins. Just to see the difference. Just to test that I didn't want to go another way," Tom confessed.

"When my father found out a couple of years later, he just about had a fit," Tom laughed.

"He wants me to take over the firm one day. I just wanted to be sure I wasn't following in Dad's footsteps because he said so." Tom ducked his head, then slowly looked up.

"I wanted to make sure. I figured it couldn't hurt."

"What did your dad do?" Lisa asked.

"Oh, he read me the riot act and lectured me on my role in the company," Tom laughed.

"I had started working for the firm the year before. I was committed to architecture." He smirked.

"I had already made my choices to follow him in this field. And I told him so. He didn't hear it. I got treated like I was still in grade school and looking for a different field." Tom looked frustrated now.

"I am *so* glad he didn't find out until later. I might have rebelled. At least for a while."

Lisa cocked her head. "Did you do anything insubordinate? At any time after that?"

"Yes." Tom smiled. "I threw a party! An I'm-not-becoming-an-oil-painter party. My friends had a blast. My father didn't appreciate it at all." Tom smirked. "But… he no longer lectured me."

"Were you living at home at the time?

"Nope. Never moved back home after college. I knew I was going to work for him, so I got my own apartment right away."

"Have you ever used oil and acrylic together?" Lisa asked, changing the subject.

"No! It can't be done!"

"Yes, it can. You know oil does not dry for weeks, sometimes months. But acrylic dries quick, sometimes in an hour, sometimes the next day."

"Yes…" Tom drawled his deep honey-smooth voice.

"When I have a subject come to my studio, sometimes I use acrylic as the beginning base of the picture and use oil over it a day or two later to enhance the picture."

"You can do that?"

"Yes, you blend the color on the page with acrylic. Oil can change it to something else or a slightly different hue. With acrylic, I can create a sketch or do an outline, with the correct colors dropped in."

"Then you cover it with oil?" Tom's eyes danced with excitement.

"Yes!" Lisa squealed. "With the oil, I can use the same colors or tweak them to accommodate the actual subject." Someone looked over at her, and Lisa flushed. "Sorry, I didn't mean to get so caught up," she whispered.

"No. Please continue." Tom gestured his hands out in a sweeping motion and grinned. "Their loss."

"Anyway, what I love about oil is its texture. It's not smooth. You can reach out and touch it and have hills and valleys all in the same painting, sometimes making a subject stand out and look three-dimensional."

Suddenly, they began to slow down to touch down. Again, Lisa's hands began to sweat as she gripped the armrest. Tom took her hand in his and looked her in the eye.

"Tell me about the contract with Bella's," he said softly.

Lisa's dry mouth tried to form words as she looked at him, wondering why he wanted to know such a private subject. "It's just a standard contract," she began, swallowing. "Well, standard for them. New for me. They hang my pictures in the gallery for six months after the showing. And they get ten percent of every sale." She went on to explain the intercedes of the gallery and the contract, going into detail, continuing to talk rather than pay attention to what was going on.

Suddenly, they touched down.

Lisa swallowed hard and then looked at Tom and smiled. "Thank you… again." She blushed. She recognized what he did—helping her stay calm during the landing. "You may become a seasoned flyer yet," Tom teased, his voice low and encouraging.

Lisa laughed. "Right," she drawled.

Others stood to get their luggage. Tom and Lisa sat there, staring at each other, their gazes locked.

Wish he'd kiss me. Whoa! Where did that come from?

Glad she didn't say it out loud, Lisa broke the staring contest first and ducked her head.

No! I will not be shy.

Lisa looked up again. Tom was grinning at her.

"Looks like it's time to get off," he said, clearing his throat.

"Yes, it does." It was Lisa's turn to smile. She took a deep breath. "And I wasn't frightened at all on this landing. Thanks for distracting me."

"Anytime."

They changed planes in Dallas, making a mad dash through the airport to catch another first-class flight to Hawaii.

They boarded the plane, and Lisa sat next to Tom. The seats were big and accommodating. Tom grabbed Lisa's hand for the takeoff and didn't let go as they watched a movie. They whispered all the way through the thriller until they reached Hawaii.

"You said you paint for a living," he asked. "Like what? What are your projects? Landscapes? People? Why did you choose it? You must really enjoy that."

"Wow! Lots of deep questions. We'll be here all night."

"That's the idea." He grinned.

"I love what I do." Lisa smiled softly. "It's creative and fun, and I get to meet a lot of people when I do a showing."

"What other mediums do you use?" Tom asked.

"On Saturdays and sometimes Sundays, I go out to the park and do chalk paintings of people passing by. I start on something of my own and someone stops by to look. I offer to do their picture and get paid for it. I have a sign that says, *'Portraits for $50'*," Lisa answered. "Isn't that too cheap?"

"Oh no. I want the work." Lisa smiled. "Besides, chalk is an inexpensive medium, and I can do several portraits with a set of chalk for weeks, sometimes months. And it is a price that people will readily pay on the spur of the moment. And I meet all kinds of people."

"Really?"

"Yes, especially if there is a crowd.

"How did you choose that path?"

"It chose me. I have always painted or drawn. Or so it seems. Mom tells me I started coloring at age two. I've known since I was a little girl that I wanted to paint. Now I want to make a living from it. I enjoy all the arts: painting, chalk drawing, sculpturing. But painting the most. Some people think it's a waste of time, but I like it, and I am trying to make it pay the bills." Lisa took a breath. "Tell me about your job. Do you enjoy it? How did you choose it?"

"I draw too, but I draw houses and buildings and landscapes. My grandfather set up his own company, and my father expanded it. And my brother and I sort of got drafted. No pun intended. I'm the eldest, at twenty-six, my brother, then our little sisters. April is still in college. Jenny is in high school. I am expected to carry on with the family firm. I like it and can't see doing anything else anyway. How about you? Do you have any brothers or sisters?"

Even though Tom acted as nothing could touch him, she saw the shadow that dropped over his eyes when he talked about the past, felt the air around them thicken with pain whenever the subject of his family came up.

"I feel like my mother abandoned me when they divorced. I lived with my dad. My brother went with my mom," Tom confessed sadly.

Most importantly, she saw the way he looked at her. Like she belonged to him. Like she always had.

"I have two older sisters and an older brother. My parents just celebrated their thirty-sixth wedding anniversary. I'm the youngest by ten years. I was the 'little surprise.' That's why it is taking everyone so long to accept that I am going to paint and make a living from it. They all think it's a waste of time. I get so fed up with all the 'be practical,' do something real-world-like. Be a CPA or a nurse. Or office work. But I hate math, and I'm not interested in working with blood or bodily fluids. I'm twenty-four years old and have always wanted to paint, draw, and sculpt. And my family has a hard time with that," Lisa complained.

Tom furrowed his eyebrows, his mouth a firm line. "My mother always said no two people are alike and don't compare yourself to others. Don't let others decide what you should do. I'm sure you are good at painting if Bella's is looking at you."

"My family just doesn't want to accept me for who I am. Now, if Bella's will just give me a contract, maybe that will show 'em."

"Most people spend more time at their job than they do with their spouse, so you want to enjoy what you do for a living." Tom's voice grew serious. "At least that's what my dad says. Life's too short to stay in a job you don't like. You're probably a lot smarter than a lot of people still looking for their dream job. You already have yours."

CHAPTER 4

The lights in the airplane cabin were dimmed.

"Are you sleepy?" Tom asked, lowering his voice.

"No. Are you?" Lisa asked, whispering.

"No," Tom said softly. He narrowed his eyes, and in one gentle move, he leaned over and touched her chin with his finger and tilted her head up to look into her eyes. Then the stewardess walked by.

Tom pulled back, his sweet blue eyes were darker and he locked onto Lisa's. He leaned forward and touched his forehead to hers. He couldn't breathe. She lifted her hand and held onto his bicep. Both breathed heavily. The lights were low, and everyone else was asleep.

Who is going to break this staring contest? Tom wondered.

He got his answer when she glanced down and then back up. Tom smiled.

Lisa lifted her head and inhaled deeply.

Sitting back, Tom broke the silence. "Tell me more about your family. What's it like having parents that never divorced?"

"Oh, sometimes it feels like a curse and other times a blessing. Half of my friends have divorced parents. It's nice that mine are married. Don't get me wrong, they disagree, sometimes at the top of their lungs. But before long, they are talking civilly again and hugging… and kissing." Lisa grinned. "If you don't mind, what happened to your parents?"

"They got divorced when I was twelve," Tom recalled.

"They fought over everything. It made me wonder why they ever got married in the first place." His thoughts seemed mindful.

"Makes a person wonder if marriage is a good thing or not." His voice trailed off.

"Oh? Are you saying marriage is a bad thing?" she finally asked. Lisa's worried look concerned Tom.

Tom gave her a big smile. He didn't feel because he didn't know anymore if marriage was for him.

"Well, for some people, it may be a good thing. Just not sure it's in the cards for me." Tom forced a fake smile. "But let's move on to a more pleasant subject."

"Tell me something about yourself that most people don't know," Lisa said. Tom leaned forward, a slow grin spreading across his face. "What *exactly* do you want to know?"

Lisa tapped a finger against her luscious lips, her eyes wide with curiosity. "Do you snore?"

Tom tipped his head back and laughed. "That's your big question?"

"I don't know." Lisa smiled shyly. "I couldn't think of anything else to ask."

Tom chuckled. He had not laughed so much in such a long time. His face hurt from laughing and smiling. He loved the way Lisa laughed, like the sound of water skipping over rocks, the sound of bells tinkling in the breeze. He wanted to listen to her laughter for the rest of his life.

"You still didn't answer my question," she declared.

"What question?" he asked, coming back to reality. Tom's eyes widened innocently, and his hand came to the middle of his chest to show surprise at being caught. "What did you ask me again?" He had been fantasizing and forgot the question.

"Do you snore, silly?"

"Well, I don't think I snore. If so, I think my friends would have busted me long before this. But if you want to verify it, you can let me know when I slip up and nap in front of you on this plane," Tom chuckled.

Lisa's cheeks flushed.

Tom loved catching her off guard and rattled. The thought of her blush got Tom excited.

She smiled back at Tom, her eyes now full of mischief. "Oh, if you *do* slip up and fall asleep in front of me…" Lisa's smiled widened, her blue eyes twinkled. "I know just what I'll do to get even."

"And what's that?"

"I'll put your fingers in an ice-cold cup of water."

Tom held his hand over his mouth to keep from howling.

Lisa giggled. Tom tried to figure Lisa out most of the trip. He thought it was cute that at times, she was shy and insecure and so scared of the take-offs and landings. But once that was over, she could make witty comments that gave the conversations playful energy. Sometimes between the jokes, there were a few moments in-between where her sense of humor fell aside long enough for Tom to catch a glimpse of a deeper, more complicated woman. They'd tackled several serious discussions, but it usually didn't take long for Lisa to bring it back to a lighter tone. And when she did, she would be jittery, but sexy as hell.

* * *

Tom watched as Lisa stared at the long winding conveyor belt in the Kahului Airport baggage claim in Maui. The bags continued to slide down the cold plastic strips that covered the chute opening and circle back around and around. Everyone else had their bags, but her bag did not show up.

Lisa had told him earlier that her bridesmaid dress was in there. So were all her clothes and toiletries. He stood with her at the terminal turntable until it was empty and the airport was almost empty too. They stared at each other with concern.

"Where do we go to make a claim for luggage that doesn't show up?" Olive stepped up and asked the attendant checking the bags against the claim tickets. When she pointed at an office, Tom stepped up and said, "I'll go with Lisa. We'll catch a later taxi."

Lisa looked at him, her blue eyes wide. He imagined he could hear her heart pounding in her chest, like a beating drum because she was worried about her suitcase. He figured she was worried about why he wanted to stay with her on this drudgery trip. His protective instinct seemed to come out, and he wanted to help. They went to the claims office to report her missing luggage, which took forever. The forms were long and detailed, but they finally closed the door to the claims office and stood outside.

Tom reached for Lisa's hand. "Ready?" he asked.

Lisa nodded and returned his easy smile.

His senses alternated between excitement and nervousness. Why was he nervous? He was *never* nervous. Especially around lovely ladies. But she was different. He was still there. And smiling at her.

His fingers lingered on the warm sensation of Lisa's hand firmly in his grasp. When they got to the sliding glass doors, Tom released her hand and placed his hand at the small of her back to usher Lisa through the doors and up the sidewalk. He smiled down at her as they walked along the pavement to the taxi stand and stood in line for the next one.

"What am I going to do for clothes till my suitcase gets here?" Lisa wailed. "Will they ever find it? Or is it lost for good?"

"We could go shopping," Tom blurted out without thinking. "Get a souvenir dress or a T-shirt and shorts." Tom dragged his suitcase behind them. "Or wait and see how long it takes the suitcase to be returned."

"You heard the lady. *If* it is returned, it may take twenty-four hours or longer."

With the extra time spent getting her bag registered as lost, it was already 2AM before Lisa and Tom got to the hotel. Olive had texted the hotel name and Lisa and Tom's room numbers, and they were already registered. They just had to pick up the key card at the front desk. Since Olive was picking up the tab, the women had a suite. The men had a separate suite. After the wedding, Olive and Mason would occupy the honeymoon suite on the top floor.

Lisa and Tom rode the elevator up to the eighth floor. Tom escorted her to the suite.

Lisa stopped at the door and looked up at Tom. "Thank you for staying with me through this fiasco."

"No problem," Tom said. He could feel the heat in his eyes and elsewhere. "We're just next door." He leaned toward her, then brushed a strand of hair slowly from her face and tucked it behind her ear. She smiled sweetly.

His hand cupped her face.

She breathed deeply.

He looked deeply into her eyes.

But then, a door slammed somewhere.

Lisa was startled and took a step back. Tom flinched. Just as quickly though, he smiled, then he took her hand, turned it over, and kissed her knuckles.

Lisa blushed. Tom really liked making her blush.

"Well, I'll see you in the morning," Tom said.

"You mean later this morning," Lisa smiled shyly.

"Right."

"Of course. Good night… or good morning."

CHAPTER 5

"You guys get lost last night?" Emma teased Lisa the next morning.

"We came straight here," Lisa answered, deliberately looking confused. "I didn't want to wake you up."

Last night, Lisa found the only empty room. Hers was the one with the door standing wide open.

"It did take a while," Lisa offered. "It was after two before we got here," she said, yawning.

"Olive ordered us some breakfast," Sophia shouted as someone knocked on the door.

The server wheeled the cart into the grand living room area. He moved the trays to the table. There were croissants, cinnamon rolls, strawberries, melons, watermelon balls, juices, and coffee. The hotel suite had a sprawling living room with a flat-screen TV behind an armoire over a fireplace and a grand piano in the corner next to the floor-to-ceiling windows. The room Lisa had stayed in last night was sensational. They were in a suite with four bedrooms—one for each woman. Olive knew how to live. Olive's father was an oil VP and her mother had old money. They lived very well. Olive had insisted that the buddy moon was on her dime. And the opulence showed.

"What are we doing today?" Sophia asked with a mouthful of croissant.

"First, we're checking on Lisa's suitcase again," Olive stated. "The maid of honor needs a dress."

"I'll call the airline," Lisa spoke up, her own mouth filled with strawberries. Swallowing, she picked up the house phone and began dialing. "I'm on hold."

After a while, Lisa was back. "They haven't found my suitcase yet. I better go buy a dress."

"I'll pay for it," Olive offered.

"No. You've paid for enough. You could come along and help me pick out something though. It'll be an all-day trip."

Olive rented a car, and they took off on their adventure.

"Sophia, let's see that purple hair ribbon you brought," Emma said when they got to the second bridal dress shop. They had bypassed the stuffy bridal shop, which Sophia commented was for old people.

"Yes, here it is," Sophia answered. "See if they have something like it."

"What can I help you with, ladies?" the saleslady, with a shock of violently purple hair and a delicate green dress, asked as the women walked in.

"Her luggage got lost, and we need a dress to match or at least not clash with this ribbon," Olive stated.

"Oh my! That's terrible!" the leading saleslady sighed with sympathy. "You've come to the right place. Let's see what we've got!"

"What are the guys doing today while we shop?" Emma asked when the saleslady went in the back to look.

"They're getting their tuxes fitted, then going swimming," Olive answered. "Mason mentioned it when I told him we were going shopping."

Sophia wandered around looking at the other dresses on display. "Wish we were swimming," Lisa mumbled.

"You just want to wear a bathing suit for Tom," Sophia laughed.

Lisa turned red. "No. I want my luggage. Speaking of which, I need a bathing suit too or I don't go swimming." Maybe if she changed the subject, they wouldn't talk about Tom. She just wanted to think about him, not have everyone else discuss him.

"I brought three bathing suits," Emma offered. "Try one of mine."

"And blue jeans," Lisa said. "I have an extra pair of jeans you can borrow," Olive said.

"You notice she misdirected us?" Emma raised her eyebrows pointedly.

"Yeah, I noticed," Sophia spoke up, laughing.

"Guys!" Lisa begged.

"This is the only thing I have that's anywhere close to purple or lavender," the saleslady came back holding a purple dress that clashed badly with the ribbon.

"Saved by the bell or the saleslady," Sophia whispered to Lisa.

Lisa grimaced, blushing again. *Oh, if I wasn't so shy with boys.*

"Well, thank you, but I guess we'll try someplace else," Olive sighed.

"I'm sorry we weren't able to help you, but you must try Anna's. It's two blocks down the street."

"There's Anna's Formals and Flora's Fashions. We've got about seven shops in this area that sell bridal dresses and formals. Let me write them down for you," the saleslady said. She wrote the list out and handed it to Olive. "Good luck, ladies."

As she visited the sixth dress shop, Lisa slumped into a chair in the sitting area of an upscale boutique. "I don't think I can look at one more dress," she pouted. The bridal consultant gave her an exasperated yet contrite look. They had been searching all day without stopping to eat.

"Come on, Lisa. We need to refocus our efforts. That's all," Emma chirped good-naturedly. "I understand how frustrating it is to look at these dresses all morning. The perfect dress is out there someplace."

"She's right," Sophia said. "We'll find it even if we have to spend the rest of the day sorting through racks of unsightly purple gowns."

Lisa laughed. "Thanks, girls. I just don't know what I'm looking for."

"Now look at this one." Olive smirked, holding up a hideously ugly purple dress. "Don't you want to try it on?"

"No!" Lisa groaned. "Fine. I'll get back in there and keep trying on dresses."

Once inside the fitting room, she stared in resentment at all the gowns in front of her that she still had to try on. They were not the right shade of purple and too extravagant. She liked simple lines.

There is no way in heaven I'm wearing this one!

She picked up the next dress just as Olive opened the door and peeked in. "Olive! I could have been naked!"

"Whatever. Not like I haven't seen you nude before. Anyway, here." She shoved another dress into Lisa's hands. "This is the one. Trust me! It's just the right color! It matches the ribbon!"

Lisa studied the dress in her hands. "Oh my," she said under her breath. At times, it felt like Olive could read her mind. The dress was gorgeous. It was exactly what Lisa would have chosen for herself.

It wasn't the same purple as the ribbon though. The lavender shade of the dress, however, did not clash with the ribbon. She carefully put the dress on and stared into the mirror. The sumptuous gown had a square neck, whereas the original bridesmaids' dresses had sweetheart necklines. The sleeves were short and capped. The other dresses were straight with no gathers. Still, it complimented the ribbon. The neckline and sleeves were different, and the color was lovely. The back of the silk gown was open, going down into a subtle V right above the beaded applique waist. The other dresses had a high plain scooped-back neckline. It clung to all her curves in the right way.

Total silence greeted Lisa as she stepped out and twirled in a circle. "It's perfect!" she exclaimed, then suddenly uneasy at the quiet.

Emma squealed, jumping up from her seat. "You're going to look better than the bride!"

CHAPTER 6

*I*t was early evening when the men walked out of their hotel room and noticed the women standing in the hall waiting for dinner. They then rode the elevator to the first floor.

"Shall we try the restaurant here or someplace down the street tonight?" Lisa asked. When no one answered, she continued, "There will be other nights, you know. We're here for two weeks after all."

"Let's eat here and scout the area tomorrow," Noah suggested, nodding to Tom.

"Sounds good. Let's go," Tom said.

Olive and Mason were snuggling rather than listening to the conversation.

Tom reached over and slapped Mason on the back. "Come on, lovebirds!"

Mason grinned.

The group entered the restaurant and were seated shortly afterward. Tom managed to sit by Lisa. She ducked her head and pushed a wisp of hair behind her ear. She shivered. *Maybe a nervous habit?*

He liked that. She was so shy.

No need to be. She's beautiful.

"How was the shopping trip?' Tom asked Lisa after they ordered.

Lisa took a deep breath and let it out quietly. "It was great! I got a new dress, and it doesn't clash with the other dresses. It's different but goes with them." Lisa answered him.

"It's a good thing Lisa has a good eye for color," Emma offered.

"Or we'd still be looking," Olive sighed, interrupting.

"The new dress is a different color, but the same tint as the other dresses," Lisa spoke up.

"The tint?" Tom asked.

"Yes, it's lighter, but in the same color family," Lisa answered. "The shading, toning, and tinting. Adding black, grey, or white. The violet-purple of the bridesmaid dresses we have goes well with the lavender dress I got today. The same tint. It's not the same color purple, but it doesn't clash."

"There you go again with the color thing in your artist talk," Emma said with a big yawn. "You can tell me more about it later," Tom said.

Lisa smiled at him.

"You got your tuxes? How was swimming?" Olive spoke up, changing the subject.

"We got our tuxes fitted. No problem. We pick them up tomorrow," Noah answered, taking a drink of water.

"Swimming was great," Bill said enthusiastically.

"It would have been better with you ladies there."

"Everything is always great with Olive there," Mason ventured, leaning over and kissing her on the temple, tangling his hand in her hair.

"Do you two want to be alone?" Noah teased.

Mason just wiggled his eyebrows.

Everyone laughed.

"And here's dinner," Olive spoke up, smiling.

After dinner, the wedding party meandered down the street to see what was there. They stopped and listened to a young man with a mustache playing guitar. Tom threw a few bills into his case, and the man nodded. The group wandered through a leather shop with boots and leather chaps, each kidding about what they could do with whatever they picked up or looked at. The men and women walked through a candy shop and each got an ice cream cone. Chairs and benches were provided outside the candy shop just for eating ice cream. Most of the shops did not allow eating in them, so this was a good stopping point. After eating the ice cream, they strolled into a T-shirt shop, and Lisa bought a T-shirt that said, "Maui and Emma bought earrings."

By then, it was getting dusk and time to go back.

The group passed a bar with music coming out of it. Emma and Sophia dragged Noah and Bill in, and Lisa, Tom, Olive, and Mason lagged behind. The bride and groom started swaying on the dance floor, and Emma and Noah and Sophia and Bill paired up, leaving Tom and Lisa. Tom looked at Lisa and extended his hand. She smiled, and they entered the dance floor.

There's that electricity again, Tom thought.

Tom focused on Lisa's arms around his neck and the sweet feminine lilac scent of her skin next to his. He felt the curve of her lower back as his palm pressed her closer to him. They danced a slow dance, then a fast one, then back to slow.

"I enjoy dancing with you," Tom whispered warmly, pressing his hand into the small of her back.

"Thank you," she answered, ducking her head and blushing.

His two fingers came up under her chin and lifted her face and tilted her head up to look into his eyes. His gaze was hot and hungry. "You have beautiful blue eyes." His hand came up the back of her neck and burrowed into her silky golden curly hair. The other settled at the base of her spine. Without thinking about it, he lowered his mouth to hers, then got bumped. Tom lifted his head. He looked up and stared at Noah, who smiled.

"Come for a walk on the beach with me," Tom murmured in Lisa's ear.

"Hmmm," Lisa mumbled, non-committal. "Let me think about it."

CHAPTER 7

$\mathcal{L}$isa stretched, putting her arms above her head. She curved her lips up at the corners as she smiled to herself. She did not want to get up, but stay here in bed and remember that almost-kiss. Suddenly, she was flooded with regret that she didn't go on the midnight walk on the beach with Tom. She could have spoken up or just left with him, but she couldn't think straight. The dancing and almost-kiss swirled in her head. She'd been so indecisive, she recalled, but then, Olive wanted to return to the hotel.

She wanted to stay in bed and dream about Tom. But the wedding party needed to get up this morning anyway. There was so much to do.

The idea of seeing Tom again made her sit up with excitement. That made her want to move, to get up.

Okay. What can I wear? What would look good without being provocative? She laughed at herself. She hadn't brought anything provocative.

Then Lisa remembered she didn't have a suitcase. It was lost or floating around in the airport space of the unknown. Never to be seen again. A bridesmaid's dress that will never be worn, assuming she actually got her bag back. *Darn.* What was in there that she had to replace at home? A hairbrush, her toiletries. All those little things—mascara, makeup, hairspray—all at once. Wow! She was suddenly overwhelmed with the thought of replacing the entire contents of her suitcase. Her lips turned down, and a crease appeared between her eyebrows.

Too much to think about. Time to get up. Think about Tom. Lisa smiled to herself again. The frown turned right side up, and the crease disappeared. *Yes, let's think about Tom.* She beamed. *Time to get dressed.*

Lisa knocked on Sophia's door as she walked into the room. "Sophia! What do you have that you can share with me? I've lost everything!"

Sophia was in the middle of her bed, stretching. "Girl, don't you ever sleep? It's way too early to get up," Sophia yawned. But she sat up on the side of the bed.

"What time is it anyway?"

"Time for you to get up." Lisa smiled at her friend from fourth grade. That's when Olive moved to town, and the four of them met on the playground. They talked and played together at school, then eventually invited each other over for playdates and had been friends ever since.

"I need clothes. I can't go out in this." Lisa swept her arm down, indicating the T-shirt that she had slept in since her pajamas were in ether space.

"And I need panties and a hairbrush. I guess I ought to buy one of my own." Lisa smirked. "I need to go shopping again." She frowned, the crease between her brows back.

"How did you sleep after that hot dance with Tom last night, Lisa?" Emma teased as she stuck her head around Sophia's door.

"Doesn't anyone sleep around here?" Sophia groused to no one in particular.

Lisa blushed. "Emma!"

"Ah, give the girl a break. Tom's a hunk," Olive proclaimed around Emma's shoulder.

"I guess no one does sleep in this place!" Sophia jumped up and grabbed a pair of panties and handed them to Lisa, then she grabbed a pink T-shirt and purple shorts and tossed those over.

"Here! I'm going back to bed." Then Sophia put her hands onto Lisa's shoulders, turned her around, and shoved her toward the door.

"You can't go back to bed," Emma announced. "We have to go shopping for Lisa. She may wear our clothes, but if so, we're going to run out—and quickly. I only brought enough for one week. I planned to wash for the second week."

"Yeah," Sophia pondered. "If she buys enough clothes for a week and washes, then she'll need a suitcase or something to return home with all those new clothes. Oh, all right. I'll get dressed. Let's go shopping. Start a list, Lisa."

The women scattered to their respective rooms.

"I'll call the airline again," Lisa called. "What about breakfast?"

"It's on the way," Olive called out.

As the breakfast tray was being wheeled in, Lisa came out of her room. "My suitcase was sent to Chicago!" she grouched.

"Then we really do need to go shopping," Emma said, grinning.

After breakfast, the ladies took the rental car to the mall.

"Did you tell the guys where we're going?" Emma asked Olive as she and Mason were virtually tethered to one another now that the big day was approaching. The women were in the store looking at the clothes for Lisa to try on.

"Oh yes," Olive answered. "Mason said they would go swimming again while waiting for the tuxes and us to return. Also, they will keep an eye out for the others who are arriving today. Don't want to keep Maria waiting. You know she has a thing for Tom."

Lisa picked up a T-shirt. Now, she looked at Olive. "Really?" Her mouth went into a straight line.

"Tom doesn't return it, but she still tries." Olive looked back at Lisa. "Just a head's up. She'll be bothering him. She can't seem to take a hint."

"Just great! Competition with Maria," Lisa moaned. Her eyebrows creased, and her mouth turned down. Maria and Lisa had a running battle over everything. Lisa had tried to take a step back from time to time, but Maria just kept pushing. It all started in sixth grade when Maria was too young to tag along with Olive, Lisa, Emma, and Sophia. But Maria singled out Lisa, taking all her hostility out on her. Everything, according to Maria, was Lisa's fault even if it wasn't. When the girls were in sixth grade, there was a sleepover at Lisa's house. Maria wasn't invited because she was in third grade, too young to appreciate sixth-grade humor or games. Ever since then, Maria had blamed Lisa for everything, then Maria got drunk at that reception and started flirting with that young man that Lisa was talking to. Lisa couldn't even remember his name now. Maria wanted everything that Lisa had. Lisa tried many times to appease Maria, to talk to her, to apologize. Nothing worked. Maria was still holding a grudge, so Lisa avoided the girl whenever she could. Now, competition for Tom's attention would be added to the mix.

The women picked out clothes and toiletries for Lisa, then she found a cloth sports bag to put all these things in. The sports bag folded up into a small space just in case her suitcase showed up.

CHAPTER 8

The guests for the destination wedding arrived without a problem. No lost luggage for them.

Thank goodness, Tom mused.

Being the best man meant he had some duties to perform for Mason, like making sure all the guests were checked in and in the right rooms. That included Maria.

Damn. He was trying to forget her.

He really liked her, but she was four years younger than him. It was too much of an age difference. She was still so immature. And he was far from in love with her. He'd like to keep her in the friend zone, but she didn't want to stay there.

Back in college, Olive invited her to a party and to check out the college one weekend. She was still a senior in high school, and he, a senior in college. Maria got drunk and came on to him, but he kept it light. He saw to it that she got home to Olive's dorm and nothing happened. He had a hard time wrestling her into her bed. She was so drunk, she was falling down. He debated leaving her in her clothes but felt bad. He had removed her dress and pulled some kind of pink cat—maybe a kitten or *Hello Kitty*—T-shirt over her full-length slip. He had *seen* nothing. Didn't want to see anything. Didn't *want* anything to happen. If he'd been caught in her dorm room and they had figured out that she was underage, he could've been put in jail, but she kept cozying up to him later like something did happen. Maybe she assumed it did. He'd never considered that before.

At least she was of legal age now. Tom ran his hand behind his neck, rubbed, and sighed heavily. He had gotten Olive's parents up to their room today and all their friends and cousins to their rooms too. Now, he was waiting for Maria. She had texted him that she was on the shuttle and would be there any minute.

Tom checked his phone for the hundredth time. *How long does it take the shuttle to get here? Thirty minutes?* It had only been thirty-five minutes now. The shuttle bus was late.

Just then, the shuttle came driving up. Maria was in the front of the bus.

"Tommy!" Maria purred in a sultry voice, like they had not seen each other for years instead of the few weeks it had actually been. They now both worked in Houston, but not at the same company. Thank goodness. She was Olive's cousin. She really overdid things. Maria grabbed Tom around the neck and pressed her breasts against his chest. She tried to kiss him on the mouth, but he saw it coming and turned his head just in time. She kissed his cheek.

"Maria, it's only been a couple of months since I last saw you," Tom said, pulling her arms from around his neck.

"Yeah, but those couple of months went by so slowly. Why don't you text me back?"

"You know I have been busy at work." Tom frowned.

"Oh, don't look so sour. You know you love me," Maria beamed.

Her black hair, which was cut in a short bob, swung on her head. She was dressed in a pink cotton top and skinny light-green-blue jeans and nude high heels. Tom licked his lips. Maria was good-looking. She was kind of hot. She wouldn't take no for an answer though. He had to admit to himself he had been sending mixed messages. He had never tried to kiss her, but he had flirted with her on occasion. And had been cold and distant on others. She, however, had been consistent with her intentions. She acted as if she thought that if she pestered him long enough and presented him with the opportunity of sex, he would succumb to her wily ways. Today, he also noticed that he used to like her perfume, but now, her perfume smelled overwhelming. He now preferred the light scent of Lisa's perfume—lilacs.

Now that he met Lisa, though, he could see the difference. He was attracted to Lisa in a way that he had never been attracted to Maria. Tom grimaced. Maybe if he just came out and told her? Tom sighed again. He'd try. But…

***

"Maria, we'll always be friends…" Tom began.

"Oh, Tommy, let's not discuss such trivial things here. Let's just get along and love each other."

"Maria…" Tom smiled. "We're friends.

"Of course, we are, Tommy," Maria said. "And we can be so much more."

"And you know I don't like being called Tommy," Tom hedged, trying to change the subject back.

"But Mason calls you TJ." Maria stuck her bottom lip out in a pout, dropped her chin, and fluttered her eyelashes at him.

Tom rolled his eyes. "You can't tell Mason anything. Are you in that category? Are you going to start calling me TJ too? He calls you Mar. Shall I start calling you that?"

Just then, the driver set Maria's luggage down by her and Tom picked it up.

"Let's get you checked in," Tom suggested, "friend."

"Okay, TJ."

CHAPTER 9

The wedding started promptly at 6PM on the beach, far away from the waves washing in and out, yet close enough to hear the beating of the surf.

Lisa watched Emma and Sophia walk down the aisle toward Mason and the groomsmen. The men's tuxes were black with satin stripping down the side of the leg and on the jacket. The cummerbund was black satin. The trouser legs were rolled up so as to not get sandy. The bridesmaids' dresses were violet and hung just past their knees.

The aisle was a runner of violet carpet leading to the groomsmen and the pastor, then the wedding party stepped onto the sand. The chairs were set on the carpet so the guests did not have to go barefoot like the wedding party.

Lisa's maid-of-honor lavender dress was cut and hemmed to just past her knees to match the other bridesmaids' dresses.

The sleeves were capped. The neckline was a sweetheart style since they had to purchase it two days ago. They were blessed to have snagged a dress in the right shade of lavender and did not clash with the violet dresses. Lisa had conflicting feelings when she put on her dress. She wanted Tom to find her attractive, but she didn't want to stand out too much. She sure didn't want to upstage the bride. Being in the spotlight scared her to death.

Lisa stepped up to her spot to wait for her turn to walk, but all she could see was Tom watching her with fire in his eyes. Her heart skipped a beat. She could see his baby-blues looking directly into hers. His slow disarming smile tipped up the corners of his sensual mouth, and her pulse raced. She needed to be watching for her cue, but instead, she was looking at Tom, wanting to marry him.

Pay attention! Lisa chided herself.

The wedding planner touched her elbow. Lisa glanced down and stepped out into the aisle. She walked down the carpet that was laid for the guests and out onto the warm gritty sand. Her senses were tantalized by the smell of salt in the air. She could also smell the pig roasting in the pit at this Hawaiian beach wedding. The soft breakers washed in and out from the ocean. Tom's sensuous lips kicked up a notch in a slow, sexy smile that warmed her from the inside out.

Lisa's did too. It was strange to be all dressed up and barefoot, but here they were. Lisa made it all the way down the aisle without mishap. She let out a sigh of relief and glanced at Tom again. His face was radiant, like he knew what she was thinking.

The wedding march started, played by violins. Olive stepped onto the aisle with her father at her side. The backless wedding dress hung just past her knees with beautiful beading on the long sleeves. There was sheer lace between the shoulder and the wrist, with beading at the end. She had a scooped neckline to match the bridesmaids' dresses. There was no train. Her father's tux was just like the groomsmen, just fancier with black satin lapels and cuffs.

Mason's smile lit up his whole face. Olive smiled back. They both looked so happy. Lisa just hoped she would find someone someday to marry her. Could that be Tom? She felt the electricity. All the romance novels said there were sparks when you met *the one*. Was that really true or just hype? Lisa didn't know.

Suddenly, Mason kissed Olive and dipped her into a romantic backbend. Whistles and claps were heard all around. He pulled her back up, and Olive giggled, then he planted another scalding kiss on Olive's mouth. Just as suddenly, the groom and now-blushing bride turned around, and everyone clapped even louder.

Where was I? Lisa wondered.

Olive and Mason started walking back down the aisle, and Tom crooked his arm for Lisa to take. She blushed. Tom smiled at her as they made their way back down the aisle.

While they waited for the pictures to be made, Tom stood by Lisa.

"What do you think of the latest *Justin Bieber* song, *Don't Cry?*" Tom asked.

"Oh, I like *This is Love* better," Lisa answered.

"Really?" he answered. "Tell me why."

"Well…" Lisa stated. "I think both were written or at least launched after he was married to Hailey, but *This is Love* is so much sweeter. It actually sounds like he is in love."

"Interesting." Tom put his hand on his chin in thought. "Did you see the article online?"

"You mean the one from *Vogue*? Yes! I did. It was just fascinating!"

"Did you know they knew each other before reconnecting?" Tom asked.

"Not till I read the article."

"Hey, you two! Get into this picture!" Olive called. "We need you!"

Lisa and Tom walked over to the group picture. "Where do you want us to stand?" Tom asked.

"You stand here by the bride," the photographer said, pointing for Lisa. "And you stand by the groom." He pointed for Tom to take his place.

The photographer took several serious pictures, then he instructed them to make faces and act silly. That was the best part. After the pictures, they washed their feet off and put on their shoes before they went inside for the reception.

***

The tables were bistro-sized with tall chairs. The buffet table was decorated with pale-violet organza and gathered white organza overlay. Overhead was a soft white fabric line with white twinkling lights. The three-tiered wedding cake was decorated with pale-violet and white-layered icing. The bride and groom on top were the traditional bride in white and a groom in black with a trellis of white, pink, and pale-violet flowers layered from top to bottom. They were standing on a platform of white. The groom's cake was a single layer of chocolate cake with chocolate icing. On top was a bride holding the coattail of the groom as he was trying to dash away. Both were smiling because of the joke. The buffet table was laden as a luau with all kinds of meats including barbecue, fried chicken, and roasted pig. The vegetables were diverse in that there were zucchini and squash (fried as well as fresh), tomatoes, mashed potatoes, and a variety of potato salads. In the center of the buffet table, two single violet roses were intertwined in a bud vase with a white ribbon bow tying them together. All along the table were strewn violet rose peddles. The bar included soft drinks, water, mixed drinks, and liquor.

The DJ was spinning the records and playing the electronic songs in an assortment of fast to slow songs, and the dance floor was full. The dancing started after the bride and her father danced to their particular song, *Daughters* by *John Mayer*. Then the bride and groom danced to their special song *Because You Love Me* by *Celine Dion*. The mother of the groom danced to their extraordinary song too—*Sunrise, Sunset* from *Fiddler on the Roof*. After that, the dance floor was opened to all the guests to dance.

Tom offered Lisa his arm. "The best man and maid of honor must dance together," he said.

"Oh yes. We must." Lisa smiled and blushed, ducking her head. Then she popped it back up.

I will not be shy, she told herself.

"Your shopping trip was successful, I see." Tom nodded toward her dress. "You looked very comfortable in that dress."

"I am," Lisa answered. "We went shopping the next day for T-shirts and shorts. We found tennis shoes and socks for me to wear on our buddy moon. We even found a soft carry-on bag for me to put it all in so I can bring it home on the plane. Yes, I would say our shopping trips were very successful. The dress is extremely comfortable for a bridesmaid's dress." Lisa glanced down.

"You look very beautiful. It's striking on you," Tom said, gently lifting her arm and stepping back so he could admire her. She had on nude heels now that they were on dry land and not sand and was a little taller. She was almost eye-to-eye with Tom. Her chin came up to Tom's shoulders.

Just right, she mused.

"Thank you, kind sir. You look very outstanding yourself."

CHAPTER 10

Tom lifted Lisa's hand and twirled her like they did on that TV dance show. Lisa laughed. Tom's gut tightened, and he knew instantly that he would do anything to hear that sweet sound again—anything at all. The other dancers clapped their hands.

He looked at Lisa. She was so beautiful, so desirable. Something drew him to her. She was different from any other woman he had been with, especially Maria. She had her own opinion when they were in private. In public, she was shy and kept her mouth shut. He wanted to keep Lisa talking all day long. She could—in private. He didn't mind being in private with her. Tom sighed and smiled to himself.

Tom looked over Lisa's shoulder at a movement and locked eyes with Maria. He glanced away quickly but not fast enough. Maria was in a pink shimmering satin knee-length dress with only one slinky shoulder strap. He blushed.

Gee, I like the way Maria looked. So sexy. Tom gulped.

He didn't want to be attracted to Maria. He didn't like it. He only wanted to be her friend. He looked at Lisa and smiled. She looked more sophisticated and natural, less makeup, and he actually liked her personality better. Maria sashayed toward them in the middle of the song.

"Dance with me, Tom," Maria purred in a sultry voice.

"No, thank you," Tom said flatly, turning to look at Lisa.

"I'm cutting in anyway. Move, Lisa."

He was uncertain how to reply. "The song isn't over yet, Maria," Tom answered, frowning. *Damn.* She was being so rude, and yet she was still so attractive. He wouldn't mind dancing with Maria. He just didn't want such a spectacle.

"Maria, it doesn't work that way," Tom stated, tightening his hold on Lisa's waist and hand and pulled her closer. He blew out a puff of frustrated air.

"Tommy, you know you want to dance with me." Maria slithered her hand on his arm. "You don't want to dance with a washed-out little girl like Lisa." Lisa's mouth dropped open as she looked at Maria, horrified, confused.

Oh my god! I can't believe she just said that! Tom felt so embarrassed.

Maria smiled wickedly. The other dancers looked their way.

"You know that Lisa's dress doesn't match the other bridesmaids'," Maria needled.

"There's a reason for that, Maria." Tom squinted his eyes at her.

"And her hair looks good," Maria said.

Tom looked up, confusion on his face. She was now complimenting Lisa?

"She did the best she could." Maria smiled sadly.

Oh, she knows what she's doing. Tom fumed at Maria attacking Lisa but was so frustrated that he didn't know what to do or say. He liked Maria, sexually, and wanted her. Sometimes. But she was rude and brash. He realized he avoided her because he just wanted to be friends, but he had flirted with her in the past. He'd never asked her out, but he'd wanted to. Something always felt wrong about the relationship. He just realized he had been sending mixed messages.

"Tom…" Lisa began.

"No." He pulled Lisa closer, twirling her away. "I'm sorry you have to listen to her."

"TJ! Just one dance," Maria continued to badger, following them around the dance floor. "Lisa won't mind. She doesn't dance that well anyway."

"Lisa dances just fine, Maria," Tom spoke just a little too loud, making people turn their heads.

Maria smiled roguishly, batting her eyes at him.

He finally gave up. "Go sit down, Maria," he said, reluctantly. "I will dance with you for the next song. Let us finish this song in peace."

Again, he guided Lisa away from Maria.

"Oh yes, Tommy!" Maria purred. "You don't know what a thrill it is to dance with you!" Maria turned and swung her hips in a sultry way over to her seat.

Tom was so frustrated and confused. He found her behavior rude and obnoxious, yet he still sexually wanted Maria. A more, raw animal desire. And he wanted Lisa in a way he didn't want Maria. He wanted to make tender, sweet love to Lisa.

How can that be?

Lisa looked confused too. "Does she do this to you all the time?"

"Yep." Tom's lips were pinched in a straight line. "I'm sorry. Now I'm snapping at you. You don't deserve that."

"I thought it was because Maria and I have a history," Lisa responded.

"What do you mean?" Tom asked.

"She hates me," Lisa said. "Everything is my fault. Even if I had nothing to do with it." Lisa looked frustrated and sad.

"What happened?" Tom asked, looking down at Lisa. "How long has this been going on?"

Lisa took a deep breath.

"Ever since we were in elementary school, she has had it out for me." Lisa's shoulders sagged in defeat. "Maria was in the third grade, and Sophia, Emma, Olive, and I were sixth graders. We had a sleepover and did not invite her. She has been vindictive ever since. I don't know how to deal with her anymore. She doesn't listen to reason."

"I know what you mean," Tom answered. "She just will not listen to anything I say. She ignores it and speaks whatever she wants to believe."

The song ended.

"I'm sorry, Lisa," Tom said. He escorted her over to a table far away from Maria.

"It's all right, Tom," Lisa responded. "There'll be other songs."

Tom nodded and walked over to Maria.

Maria smiled at him naughtily, like she had him where she wanted him. "Oh, Tommy! I can't wait to dance with you!" She smiled.

"Maria, you know I like you but you must be nice to Lisa." Tom frowned.

"Why?"

"It's courtesy. Didn't someone teach you manners?" Tom hissed.

"Tom, Lisa's a bully. She leaves little ones out of her special activities," Maria accused. "She thinks she's superior to the younger people. She finally got her comeuppance. She's just a poor starving artist now." Maria smirked, wickedly.

"Why don't you give Kirk a chance? He's interested in you."

"Kirk?" Maria actually looked surprised. "He's nothing compared to you. You, Tom, are a hunk. Let me squeeze your muscle." She moved her hand so that she could feel his bicep.

Tom shook her hand away. "Not here," he whispered.

"Oooh, you'd like to meet up somewhere else so I can feel you up?" Maria needled.

"No!" Tom exclaimed. Other dancers looked their way. "Maria! Act your age!"

"Oh, Tommy," Maria purred. "I *am* acting my age. I'm old enough now, have been for the past two years. When are you going to act *your* age and ask me out?"

"Maria, you know, I really do like you, but not at the moment though. You keep picking on Lisa," Tom answered. "But I do consider you a friend. I'd like us to stay that way."

"Friends?" Maria frowned. "I told you before. I don't want to be just friends. I want more."

"Not with me, Maria," Tom said sadly. "Now this is one dance, then you leave me alone for the rest of the evening."

"Oh, if you really insist." Maria smiled viciously. "But I don't know why you would allow yourself to be hooked up with a little strumpet like Lisa." Maria lifted her chin. "She's not good enough for you. I am."

This was annoying to Tom. He tilted his chin down toward Maria, gritted his teeth angrily, and looked her directly in the eye.

"For the rest of the trip, for as long as you are here, you *will* leave Lisa alone!" Tom ran his fingers through his hair, then straightened. "And. Me!"

"Tommy, don't mess up your hair." Maria reached her hand up to smooth out the top of his hair as they danced.

Tom was embarrassed and spoke harshly. "Leave it!"

"Oh, Tommy," Maria cajoled. "You know you love me," she said, smiling.

"Maria, that act you put on for the rest of the guests about dancing was not funny. Calling me Tommy does not make me feel kindly toward you. Not one bit," Tom said. "I don't like being called Tommy and you know it, but you persist in doing so. You continue to not listen to me when I tell you we're just friends. Please listen. Why don't you find someone else to put all your affections onto? Such as Kirk." Tom was infuriated, and he didn't mince any words this time.

"Oh, Tommy. You protest too much. One would think you really can't get enough of me," Maria wheedled.

"You're not listening to me, Maria," Tom complained.

The song ended, and Tom escorted Maria back to her table.

"Thank you, Tom," Maria said. "Perhaps we can do this again tonight."

"Probably not," he answered. Tom looked up, and Lisa was dancing with someone else. He closed his eyes and sighed.

"She'll never love you as I do," Maria said to his back.

Tom turned and looked Maria in the eye. He shook his head. He stalked over to the table across the way where Lisa had been, away from Maria. Tom was livid. What else could he do? He had told Maria to leave him and Lisa alone, but Maria persisted in following him around, harassing him wherever he went. The crazy thing was that he *did* want her. Like a one-night stand, but he didn't want her as a girlfriend. No time ever felt right when he had the chance with her. Nothing with her would ever be long-term. Thank goodness she didn't live close to him or work in the same part of town. He just had to put up with her at all the functions that Olive held—this weekend and in the future.

Olive's little cousin. Tom shook his head. He wondered if he could talk to Mason. This had to stop. Especially since Lisa said Maria picked on her too. Lisa the bully? *Hmph*! If Maria's doing the picking, *she's* the bully.

Awww, Lisa, Tom pondered. He respected her morals. She would not be an easy hook-up like Maria. She was the epitome of his fantasy woman. Lisa had stunning, piercing blue eyes. She had class. Lisa had a great sense of humor. She was intelligent, sweet, and adorable. Lisa captivated him with the graceful sway of her hips. She had thick, rich-looking golden hair settling around her shoulders like a cloud of sable silk. She was turning his world upside down.

Tom smiled. He liked his world turned upside down if Lisa was doing the turning.

He, on the other hand, didn't have any morals. Or so it seemed. He had been playing around for years with one-night stands, cheating when he tried to date continually, or one-week dates. But never with Maria. He usually let the lady know the way it was—no relationships—because he didn't want anyone to get hurt when he was ready to walk away. But not with Lisa. He wondered how in the hell this one woman could push all his hot buttons. She had him tied up in knots on so many levels. Emotionally. Physically. Sexually. All because he wanted her soft and naked beneath him, in a variety of ways. He instinctively knew there would be no forgetting Lisa Collins, and not just because she was Olive's best friend. She could stimulate both his body and mind, and that was a revelation.

He didn't want her to know his background though. What would she see in him? Was he ready for a relationship? Not really. Besides, she deserved a stable relationship with a man she could depend on. Someone who, on a regular, daily basis, could be counted on. Not someone who'd never endured a long-term commitment with a woman and didn't know if he was even capable of doing so, but now, he was on the fence about that. He worried that if she did ever found out about his past, she might not approve. Or walk away from him. Could he stand that?

CHAPTER 11

Lisa and Tom danced several dances together, then Bill cut in. They danced several dances, then Noah cut in. Lisa danced several dances with different men over the night. She noticed that Maria talked Tom into dancing with her again a few times. Tom did not look too unhappy. Maria looked ecstatic. He either sat out or danced with someone else. When Lisa thought she would sit down, Tom snagged her for another dance.

"I thought I would get something to drink soon," she told him.

"Of course," Tom answered. "Do you want to get it now or after the song is over?"

Lisa smiled into his baby-blue eyes. Her heart skipped a beat. "Oh, we can finish out this song, then I really need something to drink. My throat is parched."

When the dance was over, Tom led Lisa over to the refreshment table, his hand on her back.

"Are you familiar with our schedule these two weeks?" Tom asked.

"Yes. Tomorrow, Olive and Mason will ignore us all day. We can do whatever we want. The girls and I thought we would get a pedicure in the morning, then swimming in the afternoon since we haven't had a chance because we were shopping for the first two days. The next day, Olive and Mason join us and we drive on the Hana Highway to Hana.

"Good call," Tom said. "When you go swimming, we'll join you. Just let us know when you're ready."

"Okay. Will do."

***

Tom and Lisa were lingering over the last of the wine, their stomachs stuffed to the brim with the decadent wedding dinner. After putting the ghosts of past relationships to the side regarding Maria, they'd gone on to talk about everything else in their lives—family, friends, travel, and hobbies. Lisa learned that they were very similar in a lot of ways, as far as where they put their priorities, but there were some differences as well. Tom struck Lisa as the type of guy on an adventure. He lived his life planning his next vacation or trip. Hearing him talk about his next journey was intoxicating, and Lisa found herself getting swept up in the magic of his descriptions and dreams.

Tom had gone on a safari to Kenya in April, which was one of the best times to go. He had been to Botswana, Zambia, and Zimbabwe. He had seen big cats, like the jaguar, puma, and tiger. He saw The Great Migration with zebras, water buffalos, and antelope. In Tanzania, he saw baboons, monkeys, and apes. It was an exciting trip. He'd also been to Asia, China, and Taiwan at a different time. Last October, he'd visited Japan and seen the cherry blossoms with their bright red leaves and ridden the train all over, from Tokyo to Hiroshima.

However, once she'd come out of the fantasy, a lurking question had settled into her gut. What was he looking for? If his biggest passion in life was gearing up for an escape, that couldn't mesh well with marriage and kids. Could it? Well, that depends.

"I'm only here until the end of the buddy moon, and you seem to keep… odd hours," Tom replied, smiling at her.

Lisa sipped the last bit of wine from her glass and then toyed with the stem, dancing the base along the tabletop.

"Well, I don't know how you're going to top this." Lisa gestured around the interior of the fancy wedding that she and Olive arranged. Most of the people had left already or were preparing to leave.

Tom smiled. "Oh, don't you worry about that. I have lots of ideas." The dark, promising look in his dusky-blue eyes and his half-cocked grin got Lisa's heart racing as a shiver swept over her. He looked away right before Lisa could jump across the table and capture those infuriatingly sexy lips with hers.

Emma walked up. "Lisa, Sophia, and I are going to help Olive get changed into her going-away dress," she said. "Coming?"

Lisa turned to Tom and smiled. "Duty calls," she said.

"I'll see you later," Tom said. "Say in about ten minutes?"

"Yes," Lisa answered. Turning to Emma, she said, "Let's go."

"How is it going with Tom?" Emma asked as they walked toward the changing rooms.

"Well, I guess. You guys were right. Maria has kept pestering Tom."

"He's sure nice about it, but I wouldn't want to be in his shoes," Emma noticed, her mouth pursed.

"Yes, at least she won't be going on our buddy moon with us," Lisa sighed.

"Really! Just think how nauseating *that* would be!" Emma exclaimed.

"She just won't listen," Lisa sighed.

They walked up to Olive and Sophia. "Here's the bride herself," Emma said, smiling. They entered the dressing rooms where Olive would change.

"Are you ready to get changed?" Lisa asked.

"Yes, I'm ready. Are you ready to go on the buddy moon in two days?" Olive asked in return.

"Yes, Tom and I have been discussing it," Lisa answered.

"Getting along?" Olive asked.

"Shouldn't we? After all, we're going to be together for two weeks. We better *all* get along," Lisa said.

"I can't wait!" Sophia gushed. "Bill and Noah are fun to be around."

"Sophia, you like everyone," Emma commented.
Sophia blushed. "So?"

"Let's get Olive dressed," Lisa said, interrupting a squabble about to happen. "Turn around, Olive. Let me undo your dress."

Olive's going-away dress was light-green with white strips. It had a long waist that fell to just above the hips. The skirt part was pleated and hung to her mid-thigh. She had light-green shoes that matched.

"Here we go," Lisa said as the hotel attendant came in to gather up the wedding dress and the bridesmaids' dresses. The hotel had agreed to keep the dresses in safekeeping until the women returned from the Hana trip.

Sophia, Emma, Lisa, and Olive left the dressing room to join Mason and the men. Mason had also changed into his going-away outfit of dark-green polo shirt and blue jeans. They were only going up to their honeymoon suite in the same hotel as the wedding and reception but changed anyway.

Olive and Mason started saying goodbye to the guests. They would not see any of them for two weeks when the eight people got back from their buddy moon. The guests gathered in two lines, and Olive and Mason ran through while the guests threw heart-shaped confetti at the bride and groom. And then they were gone.

***

"Come with me," Tom said, holding his hand out to Lisa as the guests started shuffling to leave. Lisa looked at him. She was gathering up the few gifts that had been brought. The invitation had said to not bring any since it was a destination wedding, but some did anyway. Olive and Mason had opened the gifts earlier. Lisa, Sophia, and Emma would keep them in their suite. Olive made arrangements to keep the gifts at the hotel safekeeping along with the wedding dress and bridesmaids' dresses.

Tom led Lisa over to one of the wedding tables and sat down.

"What are we doing here?" Lisa asked.

"You'll see," Tom answered, smiling secretly.

Eventually, a table server came over with a small paper bag. Lisa looked at it curiously. "What is this?" she asked.

"Dessert," Tom answered, sensing her confusion. "I figured we could take it to go."

"Oh?"

Lisa followed him out of the wedding venue and to the truck the boys had rented.

"Where are we going?"

Tom smiled. "A surprise."

"Really?""Yes."

He took Lisa's hand after and held it the entire time they walked to the truck. His thumb traced little circles along the back of Lisa's knuckles. It was a good thing he was leading the way. Lisa felt like she would have probably crashed into a wall or fell on her bottom if left to her own devices with the way he made her feel. Her thoughts were completely elsewhere, with no room for things like balance and coordination. She hoped he'd rip off her clothes and take her right here, right now. She ached for a kiss. Tom helped her into the rental and pulled it out of the lot and took off. He drove out to the borders of the Hawaiian city and then a little further. They slowed when they reached a rural town on the outskirts of the city limits.

"Where are we?" Lisa asked, watching the dark shapes of fences, pastures, and the occasional mailbox flash by out of the passenger window. "The middle of nowhere? Very cute," Lisa snorted. "Is this the part where I find out you're some twisted serial killer who picks his victims up after a wedding?"

"Wow. You've got that all worked out, huh?"

"I watch a lot of crime dramas."

He laughed. "Well, sorry to disappoint, but no, your theory's incorrect."

"Well, that's comforting," Lisa said with a giggle.

Tom chuckled. "I just asked the concierge's desk at the hotel for directions so we could look at the stars. I'm a city kid. Used to bright lights, traffic, noise. I think you are too. Sometimes, it's nice to get away from all that."

He turned down a gravel driveway, and she gripped onto the handle as they bounced up the drive. She craned her head around to look at their surroundings. "Are we trespassing?"

Tom laughed and shook his head. He pulled the truck off the drive, the ride smoothing as the tires rolled over the grass pasture. He parked a few feet off the driveway and turned off the engine. "I just got instructions from the hotel and followed the GPS."

"Good to know."

Tom held up the bag that he'd tucked beside him on the bench seat. "Got some room for these?"

"When did you even have time to order that?"

"You went to the ladies' room."

"Ah, right. Very stealth. I think your talents are wasted at some computer and drawing board."

Tom chuckled as he dug into the bag and pulled out two to-go boxes. "Come on." He got out of his side of the truck and hurried around to her side. He opened her door. Tom bowed at his waist. "My lady." He swept his arm out dramatically.

Lisa giggled and stepped out of the truck.

The night was warm enough to sit outside. Tom led her over to the back of the truck and dropped the tailgate. Lisa handed him the top box after he hopped up. He took it and promptly set it aside. "Here," he said, reaching out a hand. "There's a—"

Lisa hopped up beside him with a relatively graceful jump before he could finish his set of instructions.

He smiled. "Impressive, considering the heels and the dress."

"Well, the heels were a bit of a challenge. As well as the dress, but I live in jeans and actually am somewhat in good shape," Lisa started. "I do yoga daily, even here on vacation. I've exercised each morning and evening before bedtime." Lisa peeled back the lid on the box in her hand. A poof of chocolate-scented air escaped, and she stifled a moan. Whatever was tucked beneath the waxy paper inside was destined to be a slice of heaven.

Chocolate heaven. Tom opened his box. "Shit, I didn't grab utensils. Hold on, maybe there's something in the glove box."

Lisa waved his concern away. "No worries. Dessert was made for fingers. That way, you eat every last bite."

He watched with intent fascination as Lisa reached into the box, lifted a square of triple-layer cake, and slipped it into her mouth. This time, she couldn't help the moan of pleasure as her taste buds fixed on the pyrotechnics show of delight.

"Oh my god! This is to die for. Like… if you were a serial killer, I wouldn't even care as long as you let me finish this."

Tom's head dropped back as he howled with laughter. Lisa couldn't help but laugh along. "What did you get?" Lisa asked, leaning over to pull back the lid on his box.

"Raspberry cheesecake. I wasn't sure if you were a chocolate kind of girl."

Lisa snorted. "I don't think I've ever met a non-chocolate kind of girl. If I did, I'd probably think she was some kind of cyborg."

Tom's eyes danced with amusement. "Cyborg, huh? Now you're speaking my language.

Lisa laughed. "I do have some *nerd* knowledge."

"Here." He reached into the box and picked up the firm slice of cheesecake and twisted it to point her way.

Lisa's heart leaped in her chest, kicking back into overdrive as she leaned forward and took a bite off the tip. The buttery crust melted in her mouth, but it was hard to fully enjoy the decadence, with Tom's bright blue eyes watching her mouth with unmasked desire. She wiped the crumbs from her lower lip and sat back.

"That's delicious."

He didn't say a word, his eyes still zeroed in on her lips. A shiver raced down Lisa's spine, and it had nothing to do with the evening air.

"Are you cold?" Tom asked, noticing her shudder. "I brought a blanket with us from the room. It's in the cab."

"You did?"

"Yeah, just for a night like this. Here." He hopped off the tailgate and shrugged out of his jacket. Without hesitation, he stepped toward Lisa and threw it around her shoulders, their faces inches away as he secured it in place. Lisa's breath faltered as he leaned in and the subtle scent of his cedar and woodsy spice cologne mingled between them. The jacket was warm from his body, and Lisa could feel herself melting into its silky lining.

Tom's eyes dropped from searching Lisa's wide eyes to her trembling mouth. She clung to the lapels on the jacket, not daring to move an inch. His strong fingers lifted to caress her cheek, and she sucked in a shallow breath. When his fingertips traced along her lip, her eyes fluttered closed, unable to keep from succumbing to the dance of sensations and swirls of simple pleasure that swept over her. "Lisa?" Her eyes opened to find Tom staring back at her.

"Hmm?"

"I think you're incredible," he whispered, dragging his feather-soft fingertips, up the line of Lisa's jaw. He wove his hand into her hair and brought her face toward his until their lips met in a soft, sweet kiss. As Lisa sat on the tailgate and Tom stood in front of her, his lips brushed over hers slowly, letting it grow at an intoxicating pace until Lisa pulled him closer. She put her hand on the back of his neck. Her fingers explored the place where his hair was close-cut against his neck and traced down the smooth skin until they reached his collar. Tom shivered at the touch, and he moved in closer. The kiss deepened as they came together, and she parted her legs to let him get even closer. All sense of propriety flew out the window under the moonlight as he stepped into the space Lisa created for him. Her legs rested against his narrow hips. Lisa's inner thighs brushed against the rough denim of his jeans and, combined with the fiery kiss, had Lisa moaning for more. The sound echoed back to her in the dark, and when his hand wandered down the side of her neck and over her collarbone under his jacket, she gave up trying to control herself. It was too late. Tom was too enticing to leave alone.

He dragged his lips away from hers, following the trail his fingertips had blazed down the side of Lisa's neck and over the hollow place beneath her collarbone. When his tongue flicked against her hot skin, her thighs squeezed his hips tighter, and it was all she could do to keep from panting at the rush of heat firing through every vein.

"Tom," Lisa breathed into his ear, her conscious mind struggling to regain control. "Tom, hold on." He pulled away, just a few inches, his dark-blue, hungry eyes searching hers with alarm. "What's wrong?"

Lisa shook her head and sucked in a deep breath, desperate to clear her mind before she made the wrong move.

"Nothing's wrong. I just want to… take a second."

He breathed in and put his forehead on hers. "Of course. Sure." Then he took a half-step back. Lisa clamped her legs back together.

Tom leaned back and took another deep breath. "I just need a minute," he said, his voice gravely, and he exhaled heavily.

She dragged a hand through her hair, pulled the strands off her neck in an effort to cool down. She also was breathing deeply, her heart pounding. The night air hit her warm skin and she shivered again.

"Let me get that blanket," he whispered. He disappeared before she could tell him it was unnecessary. Tom returned a second later, and she hopped down so he could spread the blanket over the cold metal tailgate.

"That's better," he said, helping her back up. "You good?"

She nodded and turned to look at him full in the face. "Sorry. I just…" She bit into her lower lip hesitating. "I really like you, and I don't want this to be one night."

He arched a brow. "That was never a possibility. At least not in my eyes. I want to see you as much as I can until the end of this vacation. And then perhaps at home. We don't live far from each other. At least it's easily within driving distance."

A flood of relief spread through Lisa, as though she'd been holding a breath too long and just got a fresh breath of air. "I'd like that too. It's just… this is all kind of new, which sounds ridiculous because of course, it's not…" She paused and shook her head. "Okay, that didn't make any sense."

Tom laughed softly and placed his hand on the side of her face, his thumb absentmindedly stroking her cheek.

"I know what you mean."

Their eyes locked together, and she leaned back toward him and pressed another soft kiss to his lips.

"Thank you," she whispered, pulling away after a sweet lingering moment. Tom nodded and dropped his hand to retrieve the boxes of desserts that had been pushed to the side.

"You wanna call it a night?"

"I have a little more time," Lisa giggled.

Tom smiled. "You sure Emma and Sophia won't send out a search party? I'm pretty sure it's past your curfew."

Lisa laughed and rolled her eyes. "I think it'll be okay."

"All right. As long as I don't have to worry about Noah and Bill coming after me."

"I'll protect you. I know someone on the inside," she replied with a wink.

He laughed and handed her the box with the chocolate cake.

"I've got to try some of this. Can't let you have all the fun," Lisa said, picking another piece of cake from the box and holding it between her thumb and finger. She held it out for him, but instead of giving her his hand, he took a hold of her wrist and pulled it toward him. Lisa's lungs emptied as he brought her fingers to his sinful lips. His eyes were locked on hers as he took the piece of cake with his mouth and then sucked her fingertips between his lips, licking away any trace of chocolate frosting.

Oh, damn.

This guy was going to be the death of her.

CHAPTER 12

"Good morning, sunshine!" Lisa groaned as Sophia and Emma bounced on each side of the wide bed in the hotel room. She opened one eye and peered up into their broad smiles, their eyes alight with mischief and curiosity. "What time is it?" she croaked.

"Eight o'clock. Well past the time to be awake and telling us all about your date last night!" Sophia bounced up and down, shaking the queen mattress, as her eyes closed again.

"Come on, please! I've been dying since six o'clock!" Emma squealed.

"Six o'clock? No wonder you fall asleep at nine if you get up at six," Lisa grumbled. She buried her face into the pillow as she rolled away from her friend, which, in a queen-size bed and a person on each side of her, was almost impossible. There literally was no escape.

"Well, if you had a friend who was going out for the first time in eight years…" Emma said, "you'd be nervous and excited too." Lisa gave her a scathing look. Emma just smiled back.

Sophia laughed and shook her shoulder. "Okay, I'm going to get you some coffee."

"Fine."

She padded out of the room. Lisa rolled back over again, opening her eyes to find morning light spreading across the ceiling. A wide, unstoppable grin spread across her face as the memories of the night before came racing back to her. It had been so perfect that it was almost like remembering a dream that she wanted to hold on to and rewind. But it wasn't a dream. Tom was real. And he said he really liked her when he'd dropped her off the night before. They'd kissed good night at the door of the suite, then he promised to call her today and meet her for lunch. Lisa was already counting down the minutes in her head.

Sophia padded back in with a cup of coffee.

"You should see the dreamy look in her eyes and the dopey grin on her face as soon as you left. She totally forgot I was here." Emma smirked.

Lisa sat up and reached for the creamy caramel-colored coffee. Emma knew her so well. After Lisa pulled off a long sip, Sophia smirked.

"Sooo?"

"It was amazing! I know I looked like a starry-eyed teenager, but I don't care." Lisa couldn't hide her elation even if she tried.

"I can see that," Emma teased.

Lisa exhaled. "It was hands down the best—and hottest—date I've ever been on. He was like this perfect mix of sweet and funny and he's hot as hell, and, although he probably knows it, he doesn't have some weird egomaniac complex about it."

"You two make a very, very cute couple." Sophia grinned. I'm already imagining your babies!"

Lisa laughed and rolled her eyes at Sophia.

"And your wedding!" Emma squealed.

"Pump the beaks, auntie. It was amazing, and we are going to see each other again. Soon. Well, for the next two weeks. But I don't want to get too crazy."

"Why not?" Sophia shot back, narrowing her eyes. "I watched you spend years with waiting, planning this life that you wanted. You already know exactly what you want."

Lisa nodded. "Right. *I* know what I want. And sure, right now Tom is as close to perfect as I can imagine finding, but it was one date, Sophia. I don't know enough about him to say he's the one. That's not my style."

Sophia nodded, and her eyes dropped to her mug of coffee.

"I didn't mean that to sound like I don't believe it can happen that fast… I mean, look at Olive and Mason. They are positively nauseating."

Sophia rebounded and smiled at me. "Aren't they! I'm happy for them."

"You're seeing him again—alone—soon?" Emma asked.

"Yeah. We're having lunch together today and making plans."

Emma shrieked. Lisa smiled at her enthusiasm and stuffed down the little pit of doubt that lingered in her gut.

It was hard not to think about the fact that, in eleven days, they'd all be back on a plane to Grove. And when reality hit at home, would he have time to concentrate on her? It was pointless to agonize about it though. She needed to soak up every last minute with Sophia, Emma, Olive, and if she got more time with Tom, it would be a bonus.

"Now we need a spa day," Emma spoke excitedly.

"But I can't spend all day at the spa. I'm going to have lunch with Tom," Lisa pouted. "Let her get dressed first," Sophia said. "Then she can leave in time to get ready for Tom."

***

The women were still at the spa while the technicians worked to file, buff, and soften every last inch of their feet and calves when Lisa's phone went off. Emma cocked her head like a dog hearing a whistle. Lisa laughed and pulled the phone from her purse that was tucked in between her leg and the arm of the chair.

"Is that him?" Sophia questioned.

Lisa smiled and pushed the answer button. "Hi, Tom."

"That's her new boyfriend," Emma and Sophia stage-whispered at the same time to the technicians. Lisa rolled her eyes, but Tom's voice took her attention away from everything around her.

"Morning, gorgeous girl. What are you up to?"

"Getting a pedicure with Emma and Sophia."

"Aha. Tell them I said hi." Lisa covered the microphone and whispered over to the girls. "He says hi."

"Hi, Tom!" Sophia and Emma called back.

Lisa shot them a look and returned to the call. "They say hi."

"I heard," Tom replied with a chuckle.

"Yeah, the entire salon heard. How's Noah and Bill?"

"Doing good as always. I'm finding it difficult to focus with you running around in my head."

Lisa laughed. "That's a good line. You gonna ask if it hurt when I fell from heaven too?"

"Damn, you ruined my next one."

"I bet."

"Well, I'll have until lunch to think of something else," Tom chortled.

"I guess."

"Is that so?"

Lisa arched a brow, and a flurry of butterflies swooped through her stomach.

"Hopefully. How about I meet you for lunch in an hour?" Lisa looked at the clock.

Heck, it was eleven-thirty already!

"One hour it is."

"Where are we going?"

"I'll pick you up," Tom answered.

"Aha!" Lisa smiled. "Another surprise?"

"Absolutely."

Lisa pursed her lips playfully, secretly thrilled by the idea. So far, he hadn't steered her wrong.

"But do wear shorts or jeans and bring a bathing suit," Tom said. Lisa could hear him smile through the phone.

***

"How about a walk? Tom asked after lunch. "There's a nice park just down the block from here."

Lisa nodded at Tom from her place across the table. They'd ended up at an authentic Italian place that was small but well-loved and that love spilled into every bite.

Lisa had worn her bathing suit under her shorts and T-shirt. "I gotta work this pasta off somehow…" Lisa blushed as she realized the insinuation that could've been drawn from her reply.

Tom's velvet blue eyes glittered in the low lights, but other than a soft smile, he didn't take the bait. He paid the check while Lisa polished off the last of her merlot. The afternoon was similar to the night before, but they kept warm enough as they walked that she didn't need Tom's jacket—although he offered. They settled into a slow stroll as they made their way down the sidewalk to the park he'd mentioned.

"Oh, I'm supposed to ask if you want to meet for dinner tonight. Olive and Mason are supposed to join us," Lisa said, patting his forearm as she held onto him. "Sure," he said, smiling down at her. He loosened his arm from her hands and wrapped it around her waist, pulling her closer. Lisa breathed in his scent and let herself get lost in the comforting warmth.

"I can make that happen."

They chatted as they walked to the park, stopping to look in shop windows that they passed if something was interesting. When they stepped into the arched entryway of the city park, a silence fell over them. Tom led the way to a bench, and they took a seat.

"Everything okay?" he asked once they were settled together.

Lisa looked up at him and nodded, but the look in his eyes let her know she wasn't very convincing.

"Then what's this for?" he asked, placing a soft fingertip against the crinkled line in her forehead. "You look like you've got something on your mind."

Lisa sighed. *Damn.* "I'm just thinking about going back home," Lisa paused, gnawing on her lip.

"Aha!" Tom nodded. "Well, if you're worried about me, you should know that I'm not going anywhere. Whether you're here or in Grove and I'm in Houston, I'm not going to change my mind about how I feel about you."

Lisa was surprised and looked up at Tom. At his bold words.

Tom chuckled. "I hope that's not too forward, but I hate all the games people play. I'm not cool enough to play the stupid "wait three days," "one text for every five," or whatever else I'm *supposed* to do or say. I like you, Lisa. A lot. And I'm not going to put that away in some little box marked off-limits with a big top-secret sticker."

Words jumbled in her mind, and when Lisa couldn't gather them together to form a coherent reply, she leaned into him and tipped her face up to kiss him. He bent the rest of the way, and their lips met with an urgent but slow-burning kiss that made her wish they weren't in the middle of a public park in the daylight. They broke apart, breathless and clinging to one another. Tom tucked a strand of hair behind Lisa's ear and smiled down at her.

"I'm really happy your friend—and mine—decided to get married."

She could still taste him after one small kiss. Bees buzzed in her stomach with the idea of wanting so much more. Lisa laughed softly.

"Me too."

They spent some time eating dinner with the entire group of the buddy moon, making plans for the next day and the next two weeks, then Lisa and Tom floated around the pool, watching the sun drop slowly over the ocean horizon from a couple of innertubes, sometimes holding hands. They'd gone back inside and watched a thriller on the big-screen TV. The popcorn bowl sat between them initially. Tom loved the way Lisa scooted up close every time the music changed to a menacing, haunting pace. By the time the credits rolled, she was practically sitting in his lap, nestled under one of his arms. Tom's hand rested on her waist, and it took most of his concentration to keep from slipping his fingertips under the edge of the tight tee she'd changed into. He was dying to get his hands on her silky skin. It was pure torture seeing it on display at the pool in her itty-bitty pink bikini top and short shorts.

"Lisa, you are a stunningly gorgeous woman," Tom said, locking eyes with her when she dared to look up. They were standing in the kitchenette in Tom's hotel suite, cleaning up their snacks. He took a few calculated steps toward her. He wanted to close the space between them and take her into his arms and get back to that comfortable ease that they'd shared earlier out by the pool or on the couch while the movie played.

She tucked a strand of her hair behind her ear and nodded slightly. "Thank you," she said shyly.

"Is everything all right?" Tom forced his hands to stay at his sides and left a few steps between them.

Lisa's eyes bounced back to Tom's from whatever she'd been looking at over his shoulder.

"Everything's fine. I think I'm just finally feeling the day catch up to me."

Tom could see it in her eyes that it was an excuse. There was something she was holding back from him. Tom smiled and pocketed his hands. "That makes sense. That's probably best for both of us. We doubtless should turn in."

She started up at Tom for a long moment, and he was about to ask what was on her mind when she turned and started toward the balcony that connected the ladies' suites to the men's. Tom followed.

Lisa paused at the door of the women's suite door. "Thanks for today. It was a lot of fun and, hey, the hard part's over now, right?"

Tom chuckled, "Right, if you say so."

She raised a hand and, just as quickly, dropped it back to her side.

"Goodnight, Tom."

"Night, Lisa."

She smiled shyly as she opened her gate and slipped inside.

"If you need anything, don't hesitate to wake me."

Lisa nodded and slid the sliding glass to the room closed softly as Tom went into his neighboring suite. He got ready for bed in slow motion, his mind distracted with reflections on the day. When he finally slid between the sheets, he found it impossible to sleep knowing that the vibrant woman in the room next to his could potentially change his mind on marriage. Hopefully, she never found out about his past.

CHAPTER 13

Tom headed straight for Lisa as soon as he saw her. "How are you doing this glorious morning, pretty girl?" he asked.

She was over by the coffee table spooning in some sugar, the sun dancing on her glorious hair. He gave her a quick hug.

She shifted away from him and looked down.

"Lisa, what's wrong?"

Before she could answer, she was interrupted by a loud voice yelling out. "Aloha!"

Every head turned to see a large man with light mocha-colored skin standing by the door.

"My name is Makoa!" he continued. "I'm your tour guide."

Definitely of Hawaiian descent, he was dressed in the Polynesian costume of no shirt, a short grass skirt with bands around his arms and head. He really looked the part of the culture.

"Could you say your name again, please?" Lisa asked.

"It is pronounced '*mah-KOH-ah*.' It means 'bold man.' You have to be a bold man to drive the Hana Highway." He laughed at his own joke. "Are you ready to take this dangerous trip with me?"

"Yeah!" Emma exclaimed.

"Dangerous?" Sophia wondered at the same time as Emma's excited response.

"Woohoo!" Noah answered.

Various forms of "yes" were expressed.

"There are some dangerous crossings," Makoa responded to Sophia. "But you will be in safe hands with me." He then looked sternly at Noah. "Please be sure you do as I say and keep your hands and feet inside the vehicle at all times." Here, he almost cracked a smile. "Unless I tell you otherwise."

"Since this is a special trip directly to the Travaasa Hana Resort and Spa, we will be taking you in our smaller van. We will still have captain chairs and oversized windows. I'm your tour guide for the whole trip," Makoa stated.

Lisa looked over at Tom, and he smiled down at her.

She flushed and turned her head.

"We will leave here in a few minutes and arrive in about three to four hours. Along the way, we will tour the island scenery on the way to the hotel, then later, we will travel to other parts of the Hana Highway," Makoa continued.

"We're not going to see the entire island before the hotel?" Noah asked.

"The other scenery that we will explore later is a longer drive," Makoa stated, looking directly at Noah again.

When the group climbed into the van, Emma spoke up. "Look at these chairs," she gushed. "They are huge! I could sleep here."

"Then you'll miss the fun along the way!" Lisa laughed at her friend.

There were two chairs on each side with a middle aisle. Everyone paired up—Olive and Mason, Sophia and Bill, and Emma and Noah. Lisa sat next to the window. Tom sat next to her. He reached out and held her hand.

Lisa pulled her hand away.

"What's wrong, Lisa?" Tom asked, concerned.

Lisa frowned and turned her head toward the window.

"The Hana Highway is a 64.4 mile-long stretch of highway connecting Kahului on the western side of the island with the town of Hana in the east," Makoa announced over the loudspeaker. "It has fifty-nine bridges, with forty-six of those only one lane wide and numerous switch-backs with hairpin curves."

Tom noticed that Lisa fidgeted nervously. He reached for her hand. "Are you afraid of heights?"

"No," she gulped. "I'm afraid of plunging a thousand feet to my death," she whispered.

Tom chuckled. "That's why we left the driving to Makoa."

Lisa turned and looked at him, her eyes huge and round.

Tom felt sorry for her, put his arm around her shoulders, and pulled her close.

Lisa froze. He pulled a little harder and she gave in, melting into his side, dropping her head.

Tom put his finger under her chin and gently pulled her face up to look at him. "What's going on, Lisa? Talk to me," he pleaded quietly.

"I'm so embarrassed, but I don't want to talk about it here," Lisa answered, glancing around.

"Just don't push me away," Tom said softly.

Lisa laid her head on his shoulder and snuggled.

Tom pulled her closer and sighed.

During the trip, Makoa told funny stories and the history of the island of Maui. "Maui was a part of a pivotal change in Hawaii's history. After conquering Maui in 1795, Kamehameha united all of the islands into one kingdom. It started in 1759 when yet another battle over land was going on. This time, Kalaniopuu, a chief from the Big Island, captured Hana from the powerful Maui chief Kahikili."

The van pulled over to the Kuau Store. They were just past Paia.

"Look," Emma pointed out. "This store has a variety of delicatessen meats and cheeses."

"I am going to get a smoothie," Sophia said. "They also have a juice bar."

"How can you eat?" Olive looked at her friend in disbelief. "We just had breakfast!"

"I'm going to have a Kombucha on-tap," Bill said, walking over to the counter. Noah, Mason, and Tom, Lisa, and Olive followed him.

"Where does Kombucha come from?" Lisa asked, looking at the menu.

"Manchuria in China is commonly cited as the place of origin. It may be as old as 2000 years old," the clerk said, smiling. "It has an alcohol content of 0.5%."

"I thought it was a healthy herb tea," Olive said, looking surprised. Sophia and Emma joined the group to listen to the clerk.

"Numerous sources have claimed health benefits from drinking Kombucha, but there is little or no scientific evidence to support it," the clerk said. "It is made from the Manchurian mushroom."

"Tell us some more about Kombucha," Lisa asked the clerk.

"The drink is reported to have been consumed in East Russia at least as early as 1900, and from there, it entered Europe. Its consumption increased in the United States during the early twenty-first century," the clerk answered. "Who wants a drink?"

"I'm going to get a smoothie too," Lisa said, looking at Sophia with her smoothie.

"Well, I'm going to have a kombucha," Olive stated, smiling at Mason.

"Me too," Bill said. Noah, Tom, and Mason spoke up and agreed.

After the group got their beverages, Makoa said it was time to get back on the road. They left Paia and traveled east to Ho'okipa lookout.

"From the bluff, you can see some of the best surfing in Maui. In the winter, the waves can get pretty massive. Maui is the Mecca to windsurfers and Kiteboarders due to the constant wind," Makoa said.

Tom watched as a windsurfer took off at that moment. Up and away he went. It looked thrilling and frightening, but he couldn't concentrate because he was wondering what was going on with Lisa. She wouldn't let him get her alone long enough to talk.

They stopped at Twin Falls, which was unique and beautiful, and watched the waves crash in below. At Waikamoi Ridge Trail, they stopped for a picnic. Makoa brought out snacks, cheeses, meats, and sandwiches.

"These sandwiches are great," Lisa said to Makoa. "Did you make them?

"Oh, no, ma'am. My sister packs the lunches for the tours."

"Your sister?"

"Yes. It is hard to not work somewhere without working with your cousin, sister, or brother. The islands are small." Makoa smiled. "It's a family place."

The group got back into the van after their picnic and traveled to the Garden of Eden Arboretum where they saw a one-hundred-year-old mango tree, bamboo, and Puohokamoa Falls.

At Kaumahina State Wayside Park, they saw the beautiful view of Maui's north coast. At Honomanu Bay, they looked out at the sparkling water, and Ke'anae Arboretum was interesting with taro, bananas, and yams.

At the halfway point, called Halfway to Hana Stand, Noah bought freshly baked banana bread to share with the others. The group could see the Wailua Valley State Wayside from the Wailua Overlook. Sadly, Upper Waikani Falls had a no parking zone, so they glimpsed it as they passed by. Puaa Kaa State Wayside Park included a quick hike to a waterfall and freshwater pool.

Hanawi Falls was a fascinating sight after they passed over the bridge to Nahiku Market Place. That was quite a fun spot. Olive and Lisa picked up gifts. Emma, Sophia, and Noah tried different kinds of food.

"Taste this…" Emma squealed at Noah, handing up a portion of a pork taco. Noah smiled at Emma and let her feed him a bite of food.

At Hana Lava Tube, they needed flashlights, which Makoa handed out. The Tube was long and narrow. Tom reached for Lisa's hand as they walked into the Tube. He gently pulled her back, and they walked slower than the others. Tom turned off his flashlight and put it into his pocket. He then softly pulled Lisa close to him. She gently tried to pull away from him.

He tightened his hold. "Lisa, what's going on? Last night, we were getting along just fine. What happened?"

"Tom, not here," she started.

He cupped her cheek and kissed her with a feather-light kiss. Lisa softened toward him. He moved his hand around her neck, lightly pulling her closer and deepened the kiss.

"Hey! Lisa and Tom! Where are you?" Noah's voice rang out at the end of the Tube.

Lisa sprang away from Tom.

"Yeah! Just exactly where *are* you?" Bill's voice now rang out. "Did you get lost? Do we need to come and *find* you guys?"

In the low light, Tom smiled at her. He reached out and lightly drew her close. She relaxed toward him as he kissed her, nibbling on her lower lip, hugged her, and yelled, "No, we're just fine!" Then he whispered, "You're so beautiful. I can't resist you." And hugged her again, then he quickly kissed her deeper and turned on his flashlight. Tom started walking toward the others, holding Lisa's hand.

Kahanu Garden was a national tropical botanical garden, which was quite beautiful. As the group walked around the bushes, tropical flowers, and trees, they continued holding hands the entire walk. At the garden was the Pi'ilanihale Heiau Temple. The Temple sprawled over three acres and had taken hundreds of years to complete.

The group passed through Keanae and saw several more waterfalls. When they got to Wai'anapanapa State Park, they finally stopped again.

Just as they were pulling up to the park, Makoa said, "Wai'anapanapa State Park is 122 acres and means 'glistening freshwater' or 'water flashing rainbow hues' in the Hawaiian language. Both refer to nearby fresh water streams and sparkling pools. Both are accurate in describing the powerful contrast between the black sand beach named Pa'iloa and the deep blue-greens of the ocean."

As the group wandered over the small black sandy beach, Lisa exclaimed, "There's a cave over there!"

"There's a cave that connects to the ocean. There's also a naturally made lava arch in the water," Makoa said. The group walked around the area for a while looking at the black beach.

"It's so different from home," Olive said, shifting a handful of black sand through her fingers.

Mason leaned down beside her and raked the sand through his fingers. "Yes, it is. But it still feels like sand."

"No, it is coarser," Lisa contradicted him playfully. "The texture is different, a little thicker."

The entire group bent and sifted sand through their hands and fingers, trying to decide who was right. Then it was time to get back into the van and move on to the final leg to Hana.

"How did Maui get its name?" Lisa asked Makoa as they got back on the van to continue their journey.

"Hawai'iloa, who was an expert fisherman and navigator, named the island after his son, who in turn was named for the demigod Māui. The Island of Maui is also called " The Valley Isle" for the large isthmus separating its northwestern and southeastern volcanic masses. In the Hawaiian religion, Māui is a culture hero and ancient chief who appears in several different genealogies. In the Kumulipo, the Hawaiian religion creation story, he is the son of Akalana and his wife Hina-a-ke-ahi (Hina). This couple has four sons. Māui is one of the Kupua, which is a group of demigods. Native tradition, however, holds that Maui is not named for him directly, but instead named after the son of Hawaii's discoverer."

"Isn't Maui the one who roped the sun?" Noah asked.

"You've done your research!" Makoa said, raising an eyebrow. Because the days were too short, he roped the sun's rays to make the days longer. When the sun pleaded for life, he made the days longer in summer and short in winter. Also, the constellation of *Māui's fishhook* is known in the west as Scorpio. Maui lifted the sky because it was so low, the people couldn't stand upright. Then he and his brothers pulled the island of Hawaii from the bottom of the sea."

"There was a computer-animated musical produced by Walt Disney in 2016 made about Maui. The film, *Moana*, tells the story of a strong-willed daughter of a chief of a Polynesian village, who is chosen by the ocean to reunite a mystical relic with a goddess. When a blight strikes her island, Moana sets sail in search of Maui in the hope of returning the heart of Te Fiti and saving her people."

"Wow!" Emma exclaimed.

"Did you realize that many consider Hana and its surrounding area as the real Hawaii?" Makoa started.

"Really?" Sophia spoke up. "Why is that?"

"It is because it has remained unchanged in Hawaii's development. This small town is quiet, beautiful, and a very important place for the people of Hawaii. It is the perfect spot to stop and recharge if you are not staying days like we are. Hana has a deep, rich history that begins when the people of the Marquesas Islands first came to Hawaii. But…" he continued, "I will tell you more about the history when we take our day trips."

Makoa pulled into the turn-around driveway in front of the hotel resort and stopped. "Ladies and gentlemen, I will see you tomorrow for our sailing and snorkeling trip to Honolua Bay."

Exhausted by the long drive, Tom stumbled out of the van, relieved that bellhops would be handling the luggage. He looked forward to a refreshing shower so that he could spend more time with Lisa.

"See you later," Olive and Mason called out as they stepped into the honeymoon suite.

He had been so absorbed in thought that he had completely missed the walk from the lobby to their cottage.

***

The rest of the troupe walked along the stone pathway that weaved between the tall trees until they reached a cute cottage that looked like a gingerbread house. Birds flitted among the branches, their calls filling the air.

The porter opened the door and stepped inside.

"This is for the ladies," the porter in-charge of the women's luggage stated.

"And over there is the gentlemen's hut," the other porter pointed a little further on.

Thank God. He was ready to change out of his clothes and maybe even rest for a few minutes. It was a little more rugged than the women's cottage. Where the women's dwelling was cute and looked almost like a gingerbread house, the men's suite looked like a Hawaiian hut on the beach with many trees surrounding it.

Tom stepped quickly made his way over to the hut and stepped inside. On the walls were masculine Hawaiian spears and face masks. There were large floor vases holding stalks of palm leaves or spears scattered about. He walked into one of the rooms and called out, "I'll take this one."

The comforter was pale-green with a palm leaves pattern. There was an en-suite bathroom with a large claw-footed tub. He immediately kicked off his shoes and began to unpack. After a few minutes, there was a knock on the door. Noah went to the door.

"Ladies." He smiled. "Welcome to our humble abode," he said as he bent at the waist and swept his arm out into the room.

Lisa, Sophia, and Emma laughed and walked into the Hawaiian hut.

"How about that! Olive did great!" Emma exclaimed. "She thought of everything! She got us a sweetheart of a cottage and a masculine beach hut for you guys."

"Hi," Bill and Tom joined everyone in the living room. They also had a three-bedroom suite. "Want something to drink? The kitchen is fully stocked."

"Yes," Sophia answered.

"No," Lisa answered. "Let's go swimming in the ocean bay just outside."

The guys looked at each other. Sophia and Emma looked at each other.

"Okay," Tom said. "Let's pack a few drinks and swim till dinner. That's a couple of hours away."

"Yeah!" everyone cheered in unison and scattered to the rooms.

CHAPTER 14

They were standing in the soft sand close to the surf. They had left their shoes back with the others. Tom ran his finger down her face. He pushed a silky piece of hair behind her ear. He was caught in the pull of her gaze, unable to look away from her startling eyes that were a deep blue with the faintest hint of gold. It was like staring into a river of clean, shimmering water.

"Lisa…" Tom said. He bent forward and kissed her softly, sweetly, slowly. Moving to the side of her neck, he reached the tender spot behind her ear. He felt like his mouth was on fire as he teased her earlobe with his tongue. She moaned as if his kisses were exquisite torture. When Tom tugged her earlobe with his lips, she tipped her head to one side and closed her eyes.

He cupped one of her breasts in his big hand as he kissed his way to her jawline, working his way slowly back to her mouth. While he captured her waiting lips, Tom pulled down the bikini top and lifted out her breast. He caressed her nipple between his fingers as he dove into her mouth with his tongue.

The kiss was slow and passionate. It was the kiss of ownership and total possession. As it deepened with intensity, Lisa responded in kind, moving her body closer. Tom felt her breasts heaving against his chest, breathing with an anticipation that had always signaled a woman's willingness to move forward.

Panting, Tom lifted his head slightly to catch his breath. Suddenly, he spied an old jeep in the distance, partially buried in the sand. Pulling away slowly, he tilted his head toward the jeep. Lisa nodded, appearing to understand what he wanted, and pulled up her bikini top over her breast. Then, clasping her hand, Tom led her to the jeep.

Sunken down in the sand, the vehicle's roof was about sitting height. Tom pulled himself up and helped Lisa to the roof, making sure she was sitting as close as possible to him, then he pulled her onto his lap.

He gazed at her and exhaled. "You're the most exquisite woman I've ever seen."

When Lisa blushed, it seemed to him that she'd never heard that before. He wondered how such a lovely woman could be so affected by compliments, much less single. At that moment, he loved her even more, if that was possible. He wanted to hold her and possess her somehow.

Tom speared his fingers through her hair, tilting her head back. He crashed his mouth to hers, forceful and demanding, overtaken by the need inside him. She moaned, leaning into him her tongue mating with his just as forcefully. His mind went blank. His logic vanished. At that moment, it was just him and her. He increased the kiss, his free hand sliding down to rest at her waist. The curve of her hip teased the edge of her grass skirt. His hand wanted to go lower. He managed to resist that basic urge and instead squeezed her against him, her hip pressing into him. Fire scorched his veins and laced up his skin. She whimpered, and he nearly came undone. If he didn't slow down… he wouldn't be able to stop. He had promised he'd go slow—at her pace. If he didn't stop, it would be too late.

"Tom…" Lisa was breathless. She melted into him. Her soft curves were against his hard planes. She slipped her hands around his neck. Tom could hear the water lapping in and out and felt the soft ocean breeze caress his face. He could taste the salt in the air. He could feel the soft sand squish between his toes. Pulling her closer, he snuggled and nibbled on her ear. She tilted her head to give him better access. As they snuggled, he stroked her silky-smooth skin. She cuddled in closer, then he moved higher on her side, up her body, to the underside of her bikini top. She moaned, and he shiftedhis hand onto her breast. He couldn't help it. He raked his thumb across her nipple.

Lisa breathed deeply and pulled away—or tried to. Tom held fast. She put her hands on his chest and leaned back. Tom let her go this time. He didn't want to. She pulled herself off his lap.

"Tom," Lisa sighed sadly. "Slow down, please." She sat beside him.

"Okay," he breathed roughly.

Lisa looked down, bright red.

"Tell me what's wrong," Tom whispered. "Did I hurt you?"

"No. I… I'm not ready to go that far." Lisa's voice was barely above a whisper. "At least not yet."

"Okay. We'll go as slow as you want." He tilted her chin back up. "You're worth it. You know that, don't you, Lisa?" He looked into her bright blue eyes.

"I am?"

"Yes. Of course, you are!"

"You're not just saying that to get me to relax and go further?"

"Of course not," Tom chuckled. "Don't you trust me?"

"Actually, I do, but I'm afraid to," Lisa whispered.

"Why? Have I done something to make you not trust me?" Tom asked, turning serious again.

"Not you."

"Someone else?" Tom almost growled. "Did someone else hurt you, Lisa?" His shoulders tensed, and his jaw clenched.

"You'll never understand. You're so sophisticated. I'm not." Lisa hung her head.

"Try me."

Lisa looked up with tears in her eyes, then she dropped her head again.

"Lisa, what is it?" Tom never wanted to see her cry.

He placed his fingers under her chin and lifted it. Her face came up, but her eyes stayed down. "Look at me," he said, gently.

Lisa shivered but opened her eyes.

"Tell me," he insisted. "Please. Tell me everything."

"I'm so embarrassed," she said, glancing down.

"Keep looking at me," Tom whispered. "I want to see those beautiful baby-blue eyes. Talk to me."

"How can you say that?" Lisa pleaded. "I'm not pretty."

"Whoa! Where did that come from?" Tom asked, startled. "What's going on, Lisa? Talk to me."

Lisa sighed heavily. "When I was sixteen…" Lisa's voice dropped to a mumble.

"I'm sorry. I didn't hear that."

"I was raped," she whispered, slightly louder.

"Oh, Lisa…" Tom whispered.

"I didn't know what to do." She went on as if she didn't hear him. "I didn't understand what was going on. I told him, 'No!' but he wouldn't listen to me. I even shouted at him. He just kept coming. He hurt me! I couldn't get him off me. After weeks of not being able to deal with it, I saw a counselor. She said it was 'date rape.' I didn't know what that was, but I learned over time, and with lots of therapy, that's what had happened."

"I'm *so* sorry, Lisa. Do you want to talk about it?" Tom said with concern. He felt anger at someone who would hurt her, but he couldn't think about himself.

"No!" she shouted. She dropped her voice and whispered, "Yes." Lisa took a deep breath. "Oh, I don't know," she whimpered. "My therapist says the more I talk about it, the easier it gets."

"Then talk to me," Tom said, raking his fingers through his hair.

"Tom." Lisa looked down, her mouth turned down. Was she going to cry?

"It was years ago… a boy…" she sighed. "He was just playing me. I, uh, let him."

"No. Sounds more like he manipulated you to think it was your fault." Tom was livid. *Who did that? I'll kill 'em!* He had to calm down. He couldn't think about himself. "That's terrible," he was finally able to say. "It makes me so angry to think someone would do that to you. Men like that—"

"He was just a boy, Tom. Let it go. I have."

"No, you haven't," Tom said gently. He tilted her chin up with his fingers. "If you had, we wouldn't be having this conversation. Is that all that… did he do anything else, sweetheart?"

Lisa blanched and looked down. "He… he… he…" she sobbed. "He took my virginity."

"Oh, Lisa! I am *so* sorry!"

"It hurt. A little. A lot. I complained. I cried."

"What did he do when you cried?" Tom softened his voice, making himself calm down.

"He laughed and said, 'Of course it hurt. It always hurts the first time.'"

Lisa was back to being stoic. "He said it wouldn't hurt the second time. I said 'no way' and left." Lisa's voice became firmer. "I jumped out of the car and walked home."

"Did you tell anyone what happened?" Tom asked.

"Not at first. I was so upset. I tried to bury it. I tried to ignore it. Make it go away."

"Who was it? Is he still in Grove?"

Lisa blushed.

"He is," Tom sighed. "Who is it? Do you see him around town?"

Lisa hung her head. "I don't see him around town much. I haven't dated anyone else since then… 'till you."

Tom sat very still. "How long ago was this, Lisa?" Tom asked gently.

"Eight years."

"Oh, Lisa, sweetheart. I am so sorry you have had to deal with all this stuff." Tom felt very sad for Lisa. He was enraged at this character that had done a number on her. Was it pity? She wouldn't want that.

"Well, I have gone out on first dates a couple of times, but they never felt right."

"And do I feel right?" Tom smiled softly, dipping his head to look her in the eye. He wanted to protect her.

Lisa blushed. She turned toward him with her mouth open, then she closed it again, clearing her throat before leaning back, looking out on the ocean again.

"Sweetheart," he murmured, trying to break the tension. Tom put his arm around her shoulder and pulled her close.

What was this girl doing to him, and why couldn't he stop? This situation was so much different and deeper than past times with other girls. He liked being with Lisa.

"Ah, Lisa…" He gently pulled her back onto his lap. "C'mere, sweetheart." And she let him. He patted her back, started running soothing circles around it, and mumbled sweet words of love in her ear. He just wanted to protect her for the rest of his life.

After Lisa and Tom had sat on the jeep roof for a while, listening to the surf lap against the sand, he kissed her softly and then stood up, pulling her gently toward him.

"We should probably head back," he said, kissing her once on each cheek.

Tom looked down at Lisa as they walked back to the hotel and was struck all over again by her loveliness. Her golden hair was shoulder-length and loose, blowing around in the breeze, and her cheeks were pink from the exertion. He was awash with love for her—love, lust, and the desire to protect her from anything bad that might come knocking. He thought about his father and wondered if he felt the same powerful love for his mother at one time or for his current wife—his stepmom. He wondered if that kind of love trumped everything.

Could he do it? Be faithful? Be engaged? Be married? Forever? To her? Only her?

CHAPTER 15

When Tom and Lisa reached the campfire where the gang had been sitting outside the hotel, they discovered the gang had already gone in.

"They left our shoes outside to wait for us. What if it had rained?" Lisa scoffed, laughing.

"We would have gotten wet," Tom chuckled. "Aren't those shoes waterproof?"

"That's beside the point. They left us." Lisa pouted, looking at the shoes sitting on one of the benches surrounding the perpetual campfire site. The campfire was out for the night.

Tom turned and nuzzled his nose into her neck, near her hair. "Didn't we want to be alone?" he asked softly.

She had her back to him, and he put his arms around her stomach. Lisa turned in his arms. Now, she faced him, looking into his blue lagoon eyes. "Yes, I guess we did."

"Do you still want us to be alone?" Tom hugged Lisa close to him, full-body hug.

"Yes," she breathed.

"Good. So do I," Tom responded. "Shall we sit out here for a while longer? Or go in?"

"Oh, let's sit out here for a while." Lisa smiled. "This time, let's look at the stars."

"As opposed to the stars in your eyes?" Tom teased.

Lisa swatted at him playfully, like a kitten batting a steel ball. She smiled.

After they sat outside for a while, Tom walked Lisa to the front door of the women's cottage, hand in hand. With his other hand, he reached up and ran a finger down her face.

"You have the most beautiful face," he said.

Lisa blushed and tried to duck her head, but he caught her chin and tipped it back up.

"And I like seeing it look my way."

When he caressed her cheek with his thumb, she leaned into his palm.

"When you look my way…" he whispered. "Let me see those beautiful blue eyes." He leaned in and kissed each of her eyelids.

She fluttered them open again when he was done. "Oh, Tom," she breathed.

"Shhh…" Tom whispered softly. "We will go as slowly or as fast as you decide. No playing games. No manipulations. No sneak attacks. Just full-on open-door policy."

"All right!" Lisa whispered back.

"See you tomorrow." Tom kissed Lisa on the mouth for what seemed like forever. It started soft and sweet and turned deep and passionate, as he pushed his hips into hers and cupped her buttocks. He pulled back slowly, breathlessly. "I better go, before I forget what I promised you." Tom smiled and kissed her forehead.

Lisa turned and put the key card into the kiosk and slipped inside the room.

***

"Hey, girl," Emma called out when Lisa stepped into the grandiose family room of the cottage. "How's lover-boy?"

Lisa blushed. "He's fine," she said, trying to sound nonchalant. "What are you guys doing?"

We're watching a scary movie with popcorn!" Sophia answered.

"Want to join us?" Emma asked, sounding a little hurt that Lisa wasn't spending all her time with them.

"Sure!" Lisa laughed. "I can sleep in a week when we get home."

***

Lisa woke up and smiled, realizing it was Thursday morning. They'd been in Hawaii for almost a week, but yesterday was the best part of the trip by far. They had ridden in a van on the Hana Highway, sneakily holding hands with Tom during the ride. And that kiss in the Tube!

She thought about the walk on the beach, the snuggling, and passionate kisses.

Then, Lisa recalled the moment when she admitted her secret. She wasn't sure if Tom got it. She didn't tell all the reasons why she thought Grey raped her. She didn't want to be a victim. Instead, she wanted to be a survivor. To thrive. Someone who had conquered the trauma. Lisa refused to be a victim. Never again, she vowed.

Okay. This morning was snorkeling, then rappelling at Honolua Bay from Lahaina Harbor, and hiking on a dormant volcano. It was being the last part of the Hana Highway. Lisa was very excited about this day. And to spend it with Tom.

Would he hold her hand again? Would there be a place for them to kiss?

Lisa caught herself smiling in the vanity mirror in her en-suite bathroom. She couldn't wait to see him.

"You ready to go?" Emma called.

"Be right there."

It was early as they met the guys and Olive and Mason downstairs. After breakfast, the group headed out, with their guide Makoa, toward Lahaina Harbor.

Lisa didn't know how long they drove, but the whole time, Tom sat beside her and rubbed her knuckles. They watched the scenery and listened to Makoa's talk about Hana's history.

"Hana means 'labor' in the Hawaiian language," Makoa continued. "It's a small isolated, tropical paradise located on the eastern tip of Maui at the end of the popular Road to Hana (Hana Highway). This sleepy village is characterized by lush greenery, botanical gardens, and historical sites and churches."

Every time Lisa looked at Tom, he smiled at her. He leaned over and kissed her whenever she blushed and dipped her head.

"Hana has a deep, rich history that began when the people of the Marquesas Islands first came to Hawaii," Makoa said. "From 1759 to 1779, Kalani'opu'u of the Big Island captured and held power over Hana. Eventually, West Maui chief Kahekili surrounded him and forced Kalani'opu'u to retreat to the defenses on Ka'uiki Hill. Kahekili defeated him by stopping all freshwater flow to the hill and forcing them to surrender."

But all Lisa could think about was kissing Tom.

Like he read her mind, he leaned over and kissed her. Then winking at her, he paid attention to Makoa

Lisa could feel herself blush.

"Queen Ka'ahumanu was born in a cave in 1768 at Ka'uiki Hill. She was King Kamehameha's favorite wife and largely responsible for the abolition of the Kapu System. It was discrimination against women and the things they were and weren't allowed to do, like not being allowed to eat with men," Makoa continued. "In 1802, Kamehameha used Hana to rebuild many Heiau, which are ancient Hawaiian temples, to honor his god, Kuha'ilimoku, and went on to conquer all the Hawaiian Islands."

But Lisa could not focus on what Makoa was saying. Her mind kept jumping to her confession the night before.

What if Tom changed his mind? What if he decided that she was too pitiful? Too much a victim?

"In 1849, sugarcane was introduced to Hana via a sugar mill by George Wilfong. In 1883, there were six plantations in operation. Before this, the area of Hana and the neighboring Ko'olau districts survived by cultivating dryland taro and local fishing."

She refused to say anything about her concerns. Besides, she felt lighthearted sitting near him. The smell of his cologne now tempted her. His kisses were mind-numbing. No one ever made her feel anything like this.

As the van pulled up to the side of the road, Makoa spoke, "Kaleo, Kai, and Bane will be your guides for the rappelling. I will meet you later with the van." Tom held Lisa's hand as she stepped out of the minivan and into a picturesque park. Lush green grass met the brilliant blue sky. "This is magical!" she exclaimed. The other girls agreed.

Everyone descended from the van.

"Kaleo," Makoa announced, extending his hand to introduce the handsome Hawaiian guide. "And this is Kai and Bane."

"Aloha!" Kaleo exclaimed to the group who repeated the greeting, smiling at each other. "So you want to do some rappelling, huh? Rappelling and canyoneering are popular worldwide, and now you can experience it in Maui. It is Maui's hottest activity."

Lisa looked up at Tom, to gauge his reaction to the prospect of being tethered to the rocks by just a rope and harness, but Tom was watching her, not Kaleo. She blushed and turned her attention back to the guide.

"You will explore a rainforest preserve and its waterfalls," Kaleo continued. "You will see why rappelling ranks as the best thing to do on Maui."

"There is a warning," Bane spoke up. "Taking that first step over the edge can lead to intense feelings of accomplishment, courage, and bliss." He smiled.

"Now, let us get you in your gear," Kai said.

"Make sure as we hook you up that we are the last one to adjust your harness," Kaleo said, looking at each one in the group pointedly. "This is extremely important."

"This experience will take place on a privately-owned, secluded waterfall valley—one of the few tourist destinations of its kind," Kai said. "You can enjoy this curious mix of peace and excitement as we rappel down into wild, inspiring raw nature."

"If you feel a sense of déjà vu during this visit," Bane spoke up, "maybe that's because *Steven Spielberg* shot the opening scenes of his movie *Jurassic Park* here."

After everyone was tethered to their harnesses, Kaleo said, "Who's first?"

"Me!" Bill and Noah both shouted at once. Kaleo and the group laughed.

"Rock, paper, scissors!" Noah shouted. The boys began the ritual, and finally, Bill was victorious. Kaleo laughed again and said, "You, my fine man," Kaleo slapped Noah on the shoulder, "can be second. In this adventure, second is no slouch. I actually go first. Bill's right behind me, then you."

"Here we go!" Kaleo shouted as he began to rappel down the cliff. Bill was next as Kai made sure he was harnessed in correctly, then Noah.

"Who's next?" Kai asked.

Tom looked at Lisa and nodded. Lisa swallowed the lump in her throat and smiled meekly.

"I will, then Lisa," Tom said.

"Okay then. Let's go!" Kai said. He checked Tom's harness and then let him go, then he checked Lisa's gear. "It will be exciting once you step off," Kai told Lisa.

Lisa just looked at him, fear snaking all over her.

Now I really am going to fall a thousand feet to my death.

Yet there was an excitement somewhere buried inside her. She could feel that too.

"Step off when you are ready," Kai said.

CHAPTER 16

Lisa hesitated, then finally did it. She stepped off the cliff. The first thing was that her heart was in her throat immediately. She screamed.

It's exhilarating! It's scary!

The gloves she had on kept her hands from being scraped up and raw from the rappelling rope. The helmet helped her feel safe if she fell. This was exciting. Oh. There was a waterfall right next to her. How beautiful. The rainbow cast over and over in different colors was right beside her. She could hear the roar of the waterfall, and nothing else. It was so much fun. Lisa never expected this to be this much fun. Kaleo said it was, but she didn't believe him. Not then. Now she believed him.

When she got to the bottom where the others were waiting, Lisa was grinning like crazy. "Oh, Tom! That was so exciting!" She grabbed him in a bear hug, and Tom hugged her back and laughed.

"You liked that, huh?" Tom asked.

"Oh! Yes!" Lisa almost shouted.

"Ready to go again?" Kaleo asked.

"Again? We're not where we're supposed to be?"

"Oh, no. We still have quite a way to go," Kaleo spoke up.

Lisa swallowed, then she took a deep breath and did it again.

They rappelled for another couple of hours and finally got to the bottom and met the van with Makoa in it, waiting on them.

"Want some snacks and something to eat?" he asked.

Lisa realized she was starving. All morning on the rappelling adventure, and now, he offered food.

Yes!

They ate and were refreshed.

Lisa looked around at the lush green grass as it met the waters of a wide slow-moving river lined with majestic swaying trees. She felt calm and really wanted a nap. "Now we need to get into the van and go hiking on the dormant volcano," Makoa said. "We will go snorkeling tomorrow."

Lisa was relieved. She was exhausted. She enjoyed the rappelling, but she was fatigued from the highs on the rappelling.

The group got into the van with Makoa driving. As they drove to the dormant volcano, he told them more about the history of Hana and Maui.

"In 1926, the original Hana Highway was completed. It was a gravel one-lane road. In 1944, the Hana Ranch began with fourteen thousand acres by Paul Fagan. He shut down all sugar production at Ka'eleku in favor of cattle-ranching operations."

Lisa looked out the windows of the van and realized that there was a lot of cattle-ranching here rather than sugarcane production.

"In 1946," Makoa continued. "a massive tidal wave hit Hana, killing twelve to fourteen people and leaving 550 homeless. It completely destroyed seventy-seven homes and damaged 156 more. At this time, all the sugar plantations closed down. Later that year, in 1946, Paul Fagan opened up the Ka'uiki Inn (Hotel Hana-Maui), which is still in operation today as the Travaasa Hana Resort and Spa. Fagan, who owned the San Francisco Seals baseball team, was some of the first guests for pre-season training. He invited many journalists to document their training, which helped in creating the hotel's initial tourism buzz."

Lisa began to doze off and tuned out anything Makoa had to say.

***

As the van pulled up to the dormant volcano, Lisa stirred. She realized her head was on Tom's shoulder. Tom turned his head and kissed her forehead.

"Morning, sunshine." He smiled into her hair.

"It's not morning," Lisa protested, smiling.

"It should be. I'd love waking up next to you," Tom whispered.

Lisa blushed. Tom chuckled. "You're beautiful," Tom whispered as he nuzzled her ear.

"Come on, love birds." Emma bumped into Tom. "Let's go. Let's get off this bus and walk on this volcano. Dormant volcano."

"Now do not get too close," Makoa said. "You can still fall in. And it will be difficult to get you out. If at all. So do *not* get too close."

As Lisa and Tom and the group looked out at the first stop, Makoa started giving the history of the Haleakala volcano.

"From the bottom to the top of 10,023-foot high Haleakala is a one-hour-and-fifteen-minute drive," Makoa started. "We will drive through the Upcountry region with its products and flower farms, where you can see the many exotic proteas. The elevation at the summit is so high that if you look closely out at the expanse of the ocean, you can see the slight curvature of our planet."

As they drove to the next observation point, Makoa continued with his information. "*Haleakala* means 'house of the sun.' It has thirteen observatories and many large telescopes at the top, all closed to the public."

Noah grunted, "Wouldn't you know it. The best part is closed to the public."

Tom snuggled into Lisa. Lisa blushed even more. "Oh, well," he whispered into her ear. "We'll see something else that is just as spectacular." Lisa smiled. Tom was so positive.

"It is the clean air at this elevation that makes for good viewing and also gives us some spectacular sunrises—a very popular visitor activity. Sunsets are also great," Makoa continued.

"Here we are at the top." Makoa pulled the van to a stop. "Here, there are several locations you can find to gaze into the caldera here at the top. Here you will view numerous cinder cones, lava outcroppings, and unearthly colors. A sight that is nothing less than spectacular."

Lisa, Tom, and the group started walking around the caldera. It was spectacular. The colors were outrageous, beautiful, and striking. The lava outcroppings were something else. And gorgeous.

Lisa sighed. She felt quite satisfied.

Then Tom reached around her waist and pulled her close. "You're more beautiful than all this," he whispered in her ear. Lisa blushed. She could feel it all over her body. Tom lessened his hug. Lisa was still blushing from the tips of her ears to her toes.

The group clambered back into the van and took the route back to the Travaasa Hana Resort and Spa.

As they arrived at the hotel, a porter came out and helped the ladies out of the van. As everyone stood outside the van, he said, "Ladies and gentlemen, please come to the beach at 6PM. There will be a luau, with a roasting pig. It is already starting to cook. There will be hula dancers. And lots to eat. Come hungry!"

Lisa pulled out her phone and looked at the time. She had just enough time to get a shower and find something appropriate to wear. She and Tom lagged behind the others as they went into their respective rooms. Tom snuggled Lisa up next to the door.

"What are you going to wear to the luau? A grass skirt?" Tom smiled.

"I don't own a grass skirt," Lisa laughed.

"What if I bought you one?" Would you wear it?"

"And where would you get such a thing in the next hour—hour and a half?"

"You'd be surprised." Tom smirked. "Would you?"

"Hmmm." Lisa tapped her finger on her lips. "Maybe"

"Yes! I knew you would!" Tom exclaimed. "Your grass skirt will be delivered within the next ten minutes."

"What!" Lisa exclaimed. "I thought you were kidding!"

"Oh no! I was very serious!" Tom smiled. "Go in. Take a shower or whatever you need to do to get ready for tonight. It'll be here in ten to fifteen minutes." Tom leaned over and planted a kiss on her nose. "See you later."

Tom stepped back, lifted his hand, and caressed her cheek. "Later." He turned and left Lisa standing beside the door of the cottage. Lisa took a few minutes and finally went into the cottage where the other girls were dressing. Lisa was in a daze.

"What are you wearing, Lisa?" Emma called out as she realized Lisa had finally come in.

"It seems I'm wearing a grass skirt."

"What!" Sophia exclaimed. "Where are you going to get such a thing?"

"Steal one of the hula dancers!" Emma laughed.

"No. It seems Tom ordered me one," Lisa said, smiling. "He wants me to wear it tonight."

"Wow!" Sophia said. "This thing between the two of you has become quite the item. Quite fast. It's been only a week."

"And what a week…" Lisa mumbled, smiling and stumbling into her room.

After her shower, Emma knocked on her door. "Lisa, you might want to check out this grass skirt."

"It's here?"

"Yes, but you might want to check it out before you wear it anywhere."

"And why would that be?"

"Just get out here and check it out."

Lisa pulled on a T-shirt and shorts and came out. Emma raised the tannish-brown skirt up and looked through it.

"It's see-through," Sophia stated.

"But it's so cute," Lisa gushed.

"Boy, does she have it bad." Emma looked at Sophia.

"Really," Sophia answered.

"But I can wear shorts under it," Lisa stated, smiling.

"You sure that's what Tom had in mind?" Emma asked, smirking.

"Of course," Lisa laughed. "Why does it matter anyway? It's my decision."

"Sure he won't be disappointed? You having clothes under that thing and all?" Sophia asked.

"Oh, phuff! He'll think I'm intelligent to improvise," Lisa answered.

"Whatever you think, girl," Emma said.

"What about a top? To go with it?" Sophia asked.

"Now that takes some thinking about." Lisa pursued her lips.

"There's a gift shop at the front of the hotel you could check out," Emma suggested. "It might give you some ideas."

"I, for one, am finishing getting dressed," Sophia stated.

"Me too!" Emma said.

Lisa just stood there for a while gazing at her grass skirt, a slight smile on her face. Finally, she gathered it up and went into her room to finish getting ready.

***

The guys knocked on the door of the cottage, and Emma answered it. Everyone was in their Hawaiian outfits—the guys were wearing Hawaiian shirts and shorts. The girls wore muumuus, except for Lisa, who had on her tan/brown grass skirt and a multicolored bikini top with skinny straps.

"Oh, Lisa, I didn't realize you had such a bathing suit top. It's cute!" Tom said.

"I didn't until this afternoon. I had to get something to go with my new grass skirt," Lisa beamed. "And where, pray tell, did that thing come from?" Olive asked.

"If you weren't hiding out in the bridal suite all the time, you might be up on the latest gossip," Sophia answered.

"Yes. Tom sent this over earlier today," Emma laughed at the face Olive made at Sophia.

Tom took Lisa's hands and held them out and looked at her. She blushed. "I, for one, think she looks beautiful."

Lisa blushed even redder.

***

The luau was scrumptious. Their group sat over with the ocean to their right as the sunset colored the sky multi colors of blue, peach, and pink. They sat cross-legged and could see the Kalua pig with the apple in his mouth and all kinds of pineapple, cheeses, and fruit, such as papaya, passionfruit, guava, rambutan, starfruit, and breadfruit.

There was a variety of fish grilled over the fires the pig had been on. And fish that was Mahi, monchong fish fillet, and grilled Hawaiian poke. There were shrimp skewers, mini Hawaiian sandwiches, and surfin' nacho boards. There were chicken long rice and Hawaiian sweet potato. Lisa loved each dish and tasted as much as she could. Each person in the group had a different favorite.

And there was haupia for dessert—a very popular coconut-milk-based dessert. This was one of many desserts. Maybe haupia was Lisa's favorite.

"Let's walk along the beach," Tom whispered to Lisa as they were finishing their dessert.

Lisa looked up into Tom's eyes. She saw a heat there, and she couldn't seem to turn away.

"Let's go." Tom stood up and snagged Lisa's hand and gently pulled her up beside him.

"Where're you going?" Noah asked.

"We're going for a walk," Tom answered.

"Be good," Bill smirked.

Tom waved his hand at him in a dismissive way. Lisa blushed.

They walked quite a way and finally came upon the old jalopy that was buried in the sand that they sat on the other night. They sat down.

"How do you like your grass skirt?" Tom asked.

"Oh, I love it. I had to wear shorts under it, but hey, it's cute."

"When I saw it, I knew you'd have to put something under it. And I'm glad you found something. And a new bikini top to go with it."

"Yes, I went down to the gift shop, and there it was. Waiting just for me," Lisa laughed.

"C'mere, sweetheart." Tom snuggled into Lisa's neck. She breathed in deeply. Lisa noticed that Tom was careful to keep his hands in place, but he did kiss her deeply and kissed her neck. This time, she matched him movement for movement, their tongues meshing in an erotic dance. She slipped her hand under his T-shirt, kneading the taut muscles beneath his shirt.

"Lisa," he murmured her name against her ear. Every hair on her nape stood to attention.

"Lisa, you are so beautiful," he breathed in her ear.

"Tom, you're a shameless flatterer," she giggled.

"No flattery needed. It's the truth." He buried his face in her hair, and the smell of his spicy aftershave sent her hormones into overdrive.

No matter how deep and suggestive, kissing was all he did though. He kept his word that she would decide how far to go.

What a relief.

CHAPTER 17

The next morning, the group got up early, again, to go snorkeling. Tom was excited. He had managed to behave himself last night as promised, kissing her mouth and neck but keeping his hands still. He wanted to let her decide when she was ready to move further. They also talked about all kinds of subjects that he enjoyed—when not kissing.

After Makoa picked up the group, he drove them to Honolua Bay. Continuing his narration, he said, "Charles Lindbergh fell in love with the Hana area and people. In 1974, he returned to Hana and finished his days in paradise. His grave can be found today in Hana."

Tom had always been fascinated by airplanes and secretly dreamed of one day flying his own, yet he didn't know this about Lindbergh. He pulled Lisa closer in the van seats. The armrests could be raised, allowing them to snuggle.

"From 1974 to today, a large part of the charm of Hana is that very little has happened since then that would be newsworthy other than land and hotel changing ownership. The people of Hana have fought hard to keep Hana a pristine, under-developed home. Though development has happened here and there, they've managed to keep Hana relatively untouched."

They finally pulled up to Lahaina Harbor, a historic set of buildings, all old but well-maintained. One two-story building revealed a drugstore as well as a gift shop inside. Lisa noticed a barbershop, a beauty salon, and a café among the other buildings.

Tom, Lisa, and the group got out, and Makoa continued with his explanations.

"Here, you will sail with experts aboard the Beauty Spirit, a luxury sailing catamaran. You will cruise the beautiful Ka'anapali coastline to the breathtaking waters of Honolua Bay, one of the most picturesque snorkeling spots on this island."

"Wow!" Emma exclaimed. "It's beautiful."

"And here is your captain," Makoa continued, "Capitan Leonard Hewitt." Then, he turned slightly and introuced each member of the group.

"Ahoy, maties!" the captain saluted.

"Ahoy!" they shouted back in unison.

"Show of hands. Have any of you ever been on a sailboat?" he asked.No one moved.

"None?" He smiled.

"Sir," Bill spoke up, "I've never been on a sailboat, but I was in the Navy and spent time on a battleship."

"Great! Someone has some water experience."

Lisa raised her hand. "We girls know how to swim."

"And what about you, handsome fellas?"

Tom, Mason, and Noah looked at each other, chagrinned. "No."

"And yet, you're willing to go out on this boat and go snorkeling?" the captain said, chuckling.

"Yes," Tom said.

"You are brave men. However, you will have to wear life jackets while in the water. No exceptions. Is that clear?"

They all nodded.

Lisa leaned over and whispered to Tom, "I'll be your life jacket."

As the guys stood there getting fitted, Tom regretted that he hadn't taken that swim class in college when he'd had the chance, but he had been offered a chance to take an upper-grade architecture class instead. And he'd jumped at it. Besides, when would he need swimming other than now?

"Let's get started!" Capitan Hewett turned toward the harbor and said, "We'll be departing from historic Lahaina Harbor. Your adventure begins aboard Beauty Spirit, a sixty-five-foot luxury sailing catamaran. Relax and enjoy the sights and the sun while eating a continental breakfast of coffee, pastries, and fruit platters as we cruise up the beautiful Ka'anapali coastline to the breathtaking beauty of Honolua Bay."

"Honolua Bay is protected as a marine conservation area. It is one of Maui's most scenic snorkel spots. You will snorkel at two secluded spots popular with sea turtles, colorful fish, and vibrant coral and enjoy our free, guided reef tours by Certified Marine Naturalists, Keely and Nick. Wild dolphin sightings are also common during the journey. You just never know what you'll see, and every day is a unique experience," Captain Hewett continued.

"Once you're done snorkeling, you will feast on a delicious lunch of grilled chicken, pork, and various mouth-watering salads. Relax as we head out into the channel for a thrilling sail back to the harbor. Let's depart, ladies and gentlemen!" Captain Hewett finished.

Capitan Hewett led the way to the catamaran and helped the women step aboard. They left the shore, and the ship hands came out and set up the sail and the group settled down to watch the hands work.

Tom noticed the cook came out with platters of pastries, fruit, and coffee and passed the snack out among the group. He also observed the girls whispering together. *Wonder what they were planning.* He smiled as he heard Lisa laugh, such a tinkling sound. He wanted to hear that sound for the rest of his life. *Whoa! Where did that come from?* Well, maybe that wouldn't be *so* bad.

"Look! Did you see the dolphins jumping?" Olive shouted, pointing off the starboard side of the boat.

"There's a whole school of them!" Emma squealed.

"How many are there?" Lisa asked.

"At least twelve!" Sophia said.

"Actually, ladies…" Capitan Hewett said as he walked up. "A group of dolphins like that is called a pod. Fish are called schools. Sometimes the pod herds the school of fish into a small confined area and feed on them. But dolphins are always a pod."

"Really!" Emma said. "That's something I didn't know."

Tom, Mason, Noah, and Bill crowded up close to hear too.

"Dolphins are often regarded as one of Earth's most intelligent animals," Captain Hewett said.

"I heard that dolphins are highly social animals," Sophia said.

"Yes, they are," Captain Hewett confirmed. "They often live in pods of up to a dozen. They have also been seen protecting swimmers from sharks by swimming circles around the swimmers or charging the sharks to make them go away," Capitan Hewett said.

"How about their whistling sound? Don't they just whistle?" Noah asked.

"Dolphins communicate using a variety of clicks, whistle-like sounds, and other vocalizations," Bill spoke up, smiling at Sophia. "Dolphins also use nonverbal communication, employing touch and posturing."

"Yes, sir. Dolphins also display culture, something long believed to be unique to humans," Capitan Hewett said. "In May 2005, a discovery in Australia found dolphins teaching their young to use tools. They covered their snouts with sponges to protect them while foraging. This knowledge is mostly transferred by mothers to daughters."

*****

They sailed on the crystal-blue water into their first secluded spot. Tom helped Lisa put on her snorkel equipment. One of the hands gave them snorkel instructions. He also helped them identify each fish class to be looking for, and he provided a full-color poster to also identify marine wildlife.

Tom slipped into the water with his snorkel gear, Lisa right after him. She reached out and grabbed his hand.

Marine Naturalist Keely, stayed close to them. Nick split his time between the other two couples.

"Come on. I can float," she said. "Let me hold your hand. All you have to do is float and look down."

"Is that what you girls were planning?" Tom chuckled.

Lisa laughed. "Yes!"

Tom appreciated Lisa's help. Every so often, he squeezed her hand, not because he felt strong, but because he suddenly felt unsure about actually floating. He'd always heard that fat floats and muscle sinks. Neither he nor Lisa had any fat on them, but he knew he had lots of brawn. He'd been working at it for years. Ever since junior high, when he was bullied for being skinny, he'd been building strength ever since. He designed his architecture plans in his head as he pumped weights or ran on the treadmill—when the weather prevented him from running outside. The amazing thing was he never forgot anything about his plans. He'd forget lots of other things like dates and dinners, but not his architectural plans.

Lisa pulled his hand and pointed with the other. A sea turtle swam by, as well as pink, blue, and goldfish school. There was a vibrant fish with orange stripes on his back and green and blue stripes on its tummy. Very colorful fish.

Lisa pulled his hand again and pointed in a different direction to a vivacious coral reef with ethereal colors.

Tom, Lisa, and the group climbed aboard. Lunch was being grilled onboard as they pulled themselves out of the water.

"Smells good!" Tom said as he helped Lisa balance. She grabbed a towel and wrapped it around herself, as each of the other girls did too.

The cook finished cooking lunch and asked, "Are you ready to eat?"

A chorus of "yeses" went up.

"First plate," the cook said, handing it to Olive as she was sitting down, then he started handing out plates of scrumptious food to everyone.

***

On the way to the second secluded popular spot, they compared what they saw, who saw the strangest, most beautiful, and most otherworldly fish after they bragged about the food. The second spot outshone the first, as great as the first was. The fish seemed to be more vibrant, more unearthly, and more alien. Tom held Lisa's hand the entire time. He wasn't quite as shaky in the water during the second snorkeling spot as the first. And he really liked holding Lisa's hand.

Even when they surfaced, Tom could not let go. They enjoyed the snacks offered and stood together on the bow of the boat, taking in the breathtaking view as they slowly sailed back to the harbor.

When the van pulled up to the hotel later in the day, Tom noticed how exhausted he was, even though he had taken a nap on the way home. Lisa had slept on his shoulder. He loved it. She was so sweet. She had held his hand while they floated and snorkeled even though he didn't know how to float. She kept him steady. Not just in the water but on land too. He liked that. He leaned over and kissed Lisa deeply, and she kissed him back. His fingers lightly caressed her neck. She shivered underneath him.

"Woo-hoo! Lovebirds!" Noah yelled at them, bumping Tom in the shoulder, which caused him to bump Lisa in the mouth. She smiled and giggled. Tom knew he wasn't in trouble.

As they descended the van steps, Lisa said, "I think I need a nap before dinner."

"Didn't you just have one?" Sophia asked.

"Or were you two necking the entire time we dozed?" Olive teased.

"No!" Lisa blushed. "I was napping. I just need more." Looking at her phone, she said, "And we've got time before dinner. You don't have to take a nap. I need one. Let me know where we're going to dinner." And just like that, she scooted off to her room.

Tom chuckled to himself as Lisa scampered off, leaving all of them behind. She wasn't always shy. Like now. She had a plan and executed it whether the others liked it or not. He wondered where they could go to dinner that night. And he wondered if there would be dancing. After all, they were at a resort. There weren't a lot of choices. He'd have to check with the front desk. He started walking in that direction.

"Hey, Tom! Where are you going?" Noah asked.

"To check on dinner," Tom answered.

"You too?" Bill called, laughing.

Tom walked down to the main office.

"Is there a special place for dinner here?" he asked the front desk clerk. "Tonight?"

"Yes, we have the Shell Lounge. You will need reservations."

"Can we set up for eight people tonight?" Tom asked.

"Seven o'clock is our earliest opening," the clerk answered.

"Sounds good. Put it under Tom Jefferys, Hut 857."

"Very good, sir."

Tom started walking off, then he turned around and asked, "Do you have dancing there?"

"Yes, sir. There is a live band and a small dance floor," the clerk answered.

"Great! Will they be here after seven?" Tom asked.

"Yes, sir."

"See you later," Tom replied.

Tom stopped by the girls' cottage and knocked on the door.

"What can we do you for?" Emma asked as she opened the door. "Oh, Lisa is sleeping," she said when she saw Tom.

Tom chuckled. "That's not why I'm here. I just wanted to let you know we have reservations at the Shell Lounge tonight at seven. Dress up. There will be dancing."

"Oh! How exciting!' Emma squealed.

"Shush. Don't want to wake up Lisa before it's necessary," Tom cautioned with a finger to his lips.

"What's going on?" Sophia came up, wanting to know.

"We're going dancing!" Emma cried.

"Shush," Tom chuckled with a finger to his lips. "Don't want to wake up Lisa."

"Why don't you want to wake me up?" Lisa asked, yawning.

Tom looked at Emma, who actually looked chagrined.

"We're going dancing!" Emma finally cried, smiling.

"Cool!" Lisa responded. "When?"

"Tonight!" Sophia answered.

"Dinner reservations are at seven," Tom said, smiling.

"Oh, look at the time!" Lisa squealed. "We've got to get dressed!"

Tom laughed.

"Go away, Tom! We've got to find something to wear!" Just before she shut the door, Lisa stuck her head out and said, "Be sure to tell Olive and Mason."

"My next stop." Then Tom snaked a hand around her neck and kissed her. Hard. "See you later, beautiful."

Tom stopped by Olive and Mason's honeymoon suite and then told the guys to get ready for the night. He was still chuckling to himself at Emma's response and Lisa's kiss.

What was this girl doing to him? He needed to get a grip.

On second thought, maybe not.

CHAPTER 18

At five minutes till seven, Lisa, Tom, and the others walked up to the Shell Lounge. Lisa had arranged her hair in a ponytail. The restaurant was beautiful. It was decorated in large and small shells, round ones, flat ones, and iridescent-colored ones. Fishnets connected them all together into a mosaic of colors.

A man wearing a floral-printed shirt approached their table and said he'd be their waiter. He had dark-brown hair and brown eyes in the Polynesian ancestry. "My name is Kale, which is Hawaiian for Charles."

"Interesting," Noah said.

"Have any of you been here before?" Kale asked.

"No," Tom answered.

"Let me tell you something about Maui cuisine," Kale answered. "Maui is well-known today for its 'Hawaiian

Regional Cuisine,' which combines the cooking techniques and ingredients from the Pacific Rim, West Coast, and Hawaii. Hawaiian cuisine has long been associated with the quintessential Kalua pig, poi, and many coconut-based delicacies."

Lisa listened contently until she was suddenly breathing deeply as Tom moved his thick thigh next to hers.

"Today, however," Kale continued, "many restaurateurs and chefs have taken Hawaiian and Maui cuisines to a whole new level, incorporating both conventional ingredients and gourmet techniques into the mix. I will be back in a few minutes to take your orders," he said as he handed out the menus. When Kale came back, Tom ordered mahi-mahi, and Lisa ordered poi. The others had Kalua roast pork and Ahi poke. And they had a variety of desserts such as macadamia nuts, caramelized fruits and sugar, coconut, bananas, and chocolate.

As they finished dinner, the band began to play. Tom led Lisa out onto the dance floor and snuggled up to her as they began to sway.

After dancing for a while, the group sat down to rest for a while, then Tom and Lisa danced again.

"Are you ready to go for a walk to our favorite jeep in the sand?" he asked.

Lisa laughed. "It *is* our favorite spot. What if someone else has discovered it? They might not like us barging in on them."

"They'll just have to leave," Tom chuckled. "It's our jeep. We discovered it first."

"We did, didn't we?" Lisa said.

"Think the others will notice if we just leave?" Tom asked.

"Tom…"

"Well, they do seem engrossed over there."

Lisa glanced over her shoulder and back again at Tom. "Tom… I—" she started.

"Come on. They won't notice until much later." He leaned over and kissed her nose.

They walked out the front door of the restaurant unnoticed by their friends, who were sitting far away from the front entrance, then they passed through the hotel lobby doors and headed for the beach. Although Tom kept his shoes on, Lisa removed her sandals and carried them in her hand.

When they reached their sunken jeep in the sand, Lisa laughed, "Look, no one has noticed it!"

Tom sat down, pulling her into a slow, deep kiss. He placed little kisses on her closed eyes, then along her jaw and, finally, on her nose. Lisa couldn't catch her breath. He rubbed his thumb against her swollen lips and smoothed her lop-sided ponytail. "We're a good team, aren't we?"

"Mmm, I guess so. Why?" Lisa asked.

He kissed her gently. She savored his sweet taste. He made promises with his mouth to cherish her. She knew he could feel every small breath and gasp as her soft breasts were crushed against him.

As Lisa leaned against him, he kissed her cheeks, her nose, and her lips softly, then he nibbled her neck.

"I meant the swimming together while snorkeling," Tom said. "You know I'd never force you to do anything, right?

"Yes," Lisa answered.

"Do you trust me?"

She chewed on her lower full lip as she wiped her face. "I do."

He caught her hand and pressed her palm hard to his mouth and then his jaw, greedily savoring the contact. Shivers of cold chased down her skin with the touch of his hot mouth. When he turned her hand over and kissed a path up her arm to the soft cup of her elbow, Lisa trembled.

Tom smiled against her skin.

Who knew the inner arm could be so sensitive?

Lisa pressed closer and ran her fingers along his bristly, smoky jaw. "I'm interested in you," Lisa said.

He took a slow exhale and picked up her other hand. "Good. I'm interested in you too.""Can I ask you a question?" Lisa asked.

"Of course. Anything," Tom answered, paying more attention to her.

"Did something happen to you too?" Lisa asked.

Tom hesitated.

Lisa knew deeply-buried pain took time to share, but she had unburdened herself and didn't want to be the only one exposed.

He held her hand and looked into her eyes as he laced his fingers through hers and released a long sigh.

"When I was in junior high, I was pretty skinny and small for my age. This kid at my school decided to go after me. My dad gave me some boxing lessons, but I was no match against Hunter. I knew he had problems. He had repeated at least one grade. Anyway, he started to bring his friends along."

"Oh no!" Lisa gasped.

"We told the school. They had the rule that until you got into your home, you were on campus and school rules applied. Hunter stopped picking on me for a while, but he found out my schedule somehow and started showing up at my baseball games, karate practices, and anywhere I happened to be after school, even on weekends. One day, my dad caught up with Hunter and told him to leave me alone. Hunter just laughed, so he informed Hunter's father, who said he would talk to his son." Tom shook his head. "Nothing changed. Hunter increased his bullying and harassment. His father had spoken to him, all right, except Hunter had been told to just make sure he won."

"Oh my god!" Lisa whispered.

Tom went on as if he didn't hear her. "We got a restraining order, but it only made things worse. He wasn't supposed to be on the same field I was on, or in the same building when I was in it, or within 130 feet if we were outside, but Hunter broke the conditions time and time again. My dad and I always reported it, but nothing was done."

"How long did this go on?"

"Three years."

"What made him finally stop?"

"I took up weight lifting. It built up my muscles, and I grew a foot! It helped a lot knowing Hunter could no longer tower over me as much, but his bullying and harassment continued. He started picking on others, besides me. I was still his favorite, but I wasn't as easy a target anymore. But apparently, he also started driving erratically or drunk. Maybe he was high sometimes. He was out of control. There was a lot of gossip. I couldn't get away from him. And it only got worse. Finally, he tried to run me over with his brand-new car."

"What?!"

"I was walking from karate class to my car and heard his car barreling down on me. I was always aware of noises by then—any noises because of him. Fortunately, I managed to jump out of the way, but he was driving so erratically that he hit another car in the parking lot. There was this loud crash and then total silence. Next thing I knew, his car was on fire. I could see him pinned inside but couldn't get close enough to help because it was completely engulfed in flames. He died at the scene."

"Wow," Lisa whispered.

Tom had recounted the gruesome details in a quiet monotone. She squeezed his hand. It didn't take a genius to know that survivor's guilt was eating him up. Unlacing her fingers, she lifted his hand to her mouth and kissed his massive palm as he had done to her.

"Sounds like you did all you could do." She pressed his palm to her face. Words didn't come easily at hurting moments like this, and she had no magic to alleviate the poor man's suffering.

Lisa looked up at him. "How do you do it?"

"Do this?" He wrapped his thick hand around her nape and pulled her close. Taking her mouth, he angled his head to part her lips. He thrust his tongue in and tasted her deeply. Her heart beat double time, and she panted, trying to catch a breath. He rubbed his thumb over her lip. "You and I both needed that."

His bright eyes had darkened, his voice becoming gravelly. He was as affected by the scorching kiss as she was. "My kiss made you forget your question?" His humorous tone snapped her out of her Tom-induced fog. His spontaneous kisses and touches had kept her in a sensual haze. His eyes filled with warm appreciation.

"Great. Your timing is perfect."

He squeezed her tighter. "When we get together, you'll know that my timing…" he teased, his voice rough as he nipped her earlobe. Heat went through her like a flash fire. Her face and other parts of her body, including her arms, were burning red.

She could barely get out the words. "Tom, you're making it really hard…"

His laugh rumbled deep in his chest. "That's fair since you're having the same effect on me."

She shifted on his lap as her entire body heated in reaction. Everything about Tom was interesting. He touched the rim of her ear lightly with the tip of his tongue.

"When I'm around you, I'm always fired up and ready." Prickly chills slithered under her already-burning skin as Tom explored her ear with his tongue.

"Honey, I've been ready since I met you. Hell, since I saw you in that sweet little sundress."God, he was doing it again. Making her forget, making her want things she wasn't sure she could ever give. He was the first man in eight years she had ever dated. Some had interested her but not kept her attention. But Tom… He put his hand on the back of her neck and tugged her so close, their breaths mingled.

"Don't pull away. Talk to me, honey."

The flush on his raw-boned face and the way his broad chest heaved under his tight T-shirt made Lisa want to crawl up his body and do her own exploring. She couldn't look at him without wanting to touch him, kiss him. She shook her head.

How had this happened so fast? It was all Tom's fault for being so damned irresistible."Tom, I'm not sure this can work."

He lifted her chin with his knuckles. He searched her face. "Tell me what worries you."

"You're suddenly hot and heavy now to have sex, but you said you'd wait for me to make that decision. And you told me you were interested in more than just sex with me."

He moved her long tendrils of hair away from her neck and gently played with them. "You know I am. I keep telling you. And I'll keep telling you over and over again until you believe me. I want to be with you, Lisa. You're the woman for me."

"I don't know if I can do sex anymore. Grey was so appalling, and I haven't been with anyone since. I assume you'll be good at the sex part. It's me. I don't know if I can," she sighed. "I'm afraid. Don't we have to do dating and normal stuff like that first?"

"It won't be just me being good at sex. It will be you and me coming together. And it will be more than good. It'll be fantastic, mind-blowing, making each other happy."

Tom made it sound easy. It couldn't be that easy, or she wouldn't be so frightened.

He ran his hands up and down her arms. "I want to make you happy. Don't you want to make me happy?"

She chewed on her lower lip. She did want to make Tom happy. She did enjoy making the people she cared about happy. "I think so."

He chuckled. "Guess that's a start." He brushed her neck and glided his hand along her cheeks. "You're a very compassionate and loving woman who cares about people. I don't think we're going to have a problem caring for each other." Lisa wanted to believe Tom.

"Let's not sweat it now. We'll just keep on as we are for now." His hands went around her waist and pulled her back against his chest. "Hold on there, princess," he whispered against her ear. "When we get around to it, you'll love it, Lisa." His hot breath was against her neck and ear and caused shivers to race along her already-sensitive skin. Just hearing her name come from his lips and staring at those big blue eyes made her breath catch in her throat.

Oh, God, she thought, *don't let him take advantage of my weakness for him.*

CHAPTER 19

Tom and Lisa held hands as they got on the van back to Kahulu. Back via Hana Highway. This was the ninth day in. Just seven more days, counting today. And four days in Kauai. That was going to be awesome too. Makoa gave them more history and information about the areas they passed again. They stopped at a few places, just for fun. Like the black sand beach with its ocean cave, Kahanu Garden, the National Tropical Botanical Garden, Hanna Lava Tube, where Tom kissed Lisa again, the Halfway to Hana Stand, more state parks, the one-hundred-year-old mango tree, and the bamboo at Puohokamoa Falls.

They stopped at Waikamoi Ridge Trail for their picnic lunch. Makoa brought out snacks, cheeses, meats and sandwiches, and drinks. After several waterfalls and overlooks, the van pulled over to the Kuau Store. Almost home—well, the original hotel.

"More cheeses," Sophia pointed out. "I need more cheese. What do you have this time? And some meats too."

"I am going to get a smoothie," Emma said. "At the juice bar."

"How can you two eat?" Olive asked. "We just had lunch."

They passed Paia, and finally, they made it back to Kahului and then the airport. They flew straight over to Lihue Airport in Kauai. It was about a two-hour trip.

Olive rented a van to pick them up at the airport so all could sight-see. The van pulled up and a Hawaiian-Polynesian man with curly black hair stepped off the van.

"Aloha! My name is Pika, which means Peter, rock, or stone." He looked over each guest. "And I have leis for each of you!" He held a group of leis draped over his arm and stepped forward to place a lei over Emma's head, then he draped Sophia with a lei and Olive, Mason, Noah, and Bill. Then he smiled at Tom and Lisa's clasped hands.

"So you are the honeymoon couple?" Pika asked.

Lisa blushed and pushed a strand of hair behind her ear.

Tom tightened their hands as she tried to pull away. "No." He pointed with the other hand to Olive and Mason, who were not holding hands. "They are."

"Aha! Pardon me, ladies and sirs. Let me finish placing this lei on this pretty lady and handsome gentleman. And I will talk to you."

Pika, Olive, and Mason stepped aside to discuss the arrangements. When they agreed, the group started on their way to their hotel in Waimea.

On the way, Pika pointed out that they would catch some awesome views, especially from the scenic overlooks. Kauai was known as the Garden Isle.

Tom, Lisa, and the group enjoyed the multiple waterfalls and picturesque overlooks to the ocean, then the next beautiful scene was the mountains in the distance and the lush green landscape in between.

Tom especially liked Menehune Fishpond near Lihue, one of the first scenes they saw, close to the airport. It reminded him of one of the vacations he had taken.

"Menehune Fishpond is also known as Alekoko Fishpond or Niumalu Pond," Pika said. "And listed on the US National Register of Historic Places in 1973. It is bounded by a wall 900 yards long at a large bend in *Hulē'ia* River. It has been deemed 'the most significant fishpond on Kauai,' both in Hawaiian legends and folklore and in the eyes of Kauai's people today. It is so old that its construction is attributed to the menehunes—mythical people inhabiting Hawaii before the Hawaiians arrived. Additionally, it is the best example of an inland fishpond in the entire state."

Tom, Lisa, and the others took the paths to the bottom of the Wailua Falls. As they were walking to the falls, Tom pulled Lisa over in a little alcove along the path.

"Tom," Lisa whispered. "The others will see."

"So?" Tom said as he pulled Lisa slowly toward him and captured her lips in a soft, erotic kiss.

Lisa wound her hands around Tom's neck and pulled him as close to her as possible.

"Tom! Lisa!" Bill's voice rang out. "Where are you?"

Tom leisurely pulled away from Lisa, their breathing labored. He smiled. "I guess that's our cue."

"I guess so," Lisa answered.

"Okay." Tom moved his hand down and caressed Lisa's butt softly.

"Tom!" Lisa laughed and swatted his hand away.

"Yes?" he asked.

"Let's go. People are waiting."

Tom and Lisa caught up with the rest of the group just as Pika was explaining the history of the falls"Wailua Falls is a one-hundred-and-seventy-three-foot waterfall located near Lihue that feeds into the Wailua River. The waterfall is prominently featured on the opening credits of the TV series *Fantasy Island*," Pika said.

"*Fantasy Island?*" Emma squealed. "I remember watching that on reruns on TV!"

"Yeah," Noah agreed. "I seem to remember that show."

"In ancient times," Pika continued, "Hawaiian men would jump from the top of the falls to prove their manhood. Some people still leap off the top of the falls."

"Oooh," Mason said.

"But…" Pika paused. "It is dangerous and illegal. In 2016, a man jumped from the falls and was knocked unconscious. He narrowly avoided death when someone else swam out into the pool to save him. The pool is great for swimming, but there are swift currents close to the waterfall. There is another waterfall nearby named 'Opaeka'a Falls.'"

"We could go swimming," Sophia suggested.

"Our bathing suits are packed," Lisa said.

"Besides, he said it is dangerous swift currents close to the waterfall," Olive said. "He didn't use the word dangerous about the swimming but about jumping off the top of the waterfall," Noah spoke up.

"Besides all that," Lisa spoke up. "Our suits are still packed in the back of the van."

Tom chuckled.

"It is time to continue to the hotel," Pika said to let the group know.

"Maybe we could come back and go swimming while we are here," Emma suggested.

"Maybe," Sophia answered.

"Olive," Lisa asked. "Will we have time to go swimming at the falls before we leave here?" Olive and Lisa did all the planning of the trip.

"No," Olive answered. "We do have swimming planned for another day. Swimming and snorkeling at Tunnels Beach. We are also going to see the Grand Canyon of the Pacific."

"I thought the Grand Canyon was in Colorado?" Emma asked.

"It is." Olive smiled. "This one is the Grand Canyon of the Pacific. A different Grand Canyon."

"What else are we going to do?"

"We're going to see several state parks. Not in this particular order, though," Olive answered. "And we're going to see lookouts, waterfalls, beaches, and Hanalei Bay—the largest bay on the north shore. We're on the west shore right now. The airport is on the east side. Mountains, canyons, caves, and hiking. All in three days. Oh, and Tahitian dancing with a luau."

"Doesn't sound like we have time to squeeze in another activity," Bill chuckled.

"Here we are on the top," Pika announced. "Let us go on to the hotel."

As the van made its way toward the hotel, the group continued to discuss the coming planned activities.

Tom and Lisa sat together in the van, holding hands, occasionally kissing.

When the van pulled up to the Westin Princeville Ocean Resort, the group descended the steps.

"Oh, it's pretty here!" Emma said softly. "Look at all the beautiful flowers."

"Yes, it's gorgeous here," Olive said. "This hotel has rooms like a regular hotel, but they have cottages here too. They're bigger than the hotel rooms. And that's what we have.

"Are they like the cottages we had in Maui?" Lisa asked.

"No. More like the Hawaiian homes with open windows that have sliding glass doors to close at night because we are at a hotel, but a more Hawaiian touch," Olive answered.

"What kind of flowers are these? Do you know?" Lisa asked.

"Yes, that is the poinciana flower. It can be a bush or a tree. There was a song written about it in the 1950s by *The Four Freshmen*. It was originally from Madagascar and brought here to Hawaii."

"And the purple ones and the white ones are jacarandas," Olive continued. "It can be a bush or a tree or a flower too. It was originally from South America."

"And these are the red ginger," Olive said. "These can be red, beige, or light-yellow and are used for medical and aesthetic purposes. Hawaiian royalty once wore leis of red ginger for special occasions."

"I love it!" Lisa exclaimed. "All three of them!"

That night, Tom, Lisa, and the rest of the group walked to the restaurant in the hotel to have dinner. Lisa told Tom all about the poinciana, red ginger, and jacaranda flowers outside their cottage.

After dinner, Tom reached over and grabbed Lisa's hand. "Let's go for a walk," he said.

Lisa blushed and smiled. "Okay."

They rose and said goodnight to the others and left. Tom took Lisa's hand and led her out of the restaurant and stopped by the concierge's desk.

"Do you have a blanket or something we could sit on?" Tom asked. "We want to take a stroll along the beach and then sit and talk."

"Yes, sir. One moment please." The concierge stepped back behind the desk and into a closet he had not noticed before, then the concierge came back out with a blanket.

Tom took the blanket and slipped it over his shoulder.

"Would you like a basket to carry it in?" the concierge asked.

"That would be great. Then we could take something to drink with us," Tom answered. The concierge bent over and, underneath the counter, he pulled out a basket, just the right size to carry the blanket. He handed it to Tom.

"Shall I call the kitchen and have them bring out some drinks for you?"

Tom looked at Lisa, who smiled and nodded, then he looked back at the concierge and answered, "Yes, thank you."

"What would you like?"

"Two teas and two waters," Tom answered.

After their drinks came, Tom laced his fingers with Lisa's, and they walked hand in hand out onto the beach. It was still bright outside but late. It would be dark though when they returned.

"Do you miss painting while you are here?" Tom asked.

"Who says I'm not doing something while I'm here?"

"What does that mean? Did you bring your paints with you?" Tom chuckled.

"No, I brought my sketchbook and coloring pencils with me. I draw and sometimes put in the correct colors so I can paint them when I get home. I already have enough to paint for months." Lisa smiled. "I even drew the poinciana, red ginger, and jacaranda flowers."

"What about your phone?" Tom asked. "Don't you take pictures? I thought I saw you taking pictures sometimes."

"I also take pictures with my phone," Lisa answered. "That's really the best and fastest way to remember the areas, but I like to sketch when I get back to the room, before going to bed. Or if I get up early enough before everyone else in the morning."

"You know you can come knock on my door in the mornings," Tom suggested. "I like getting up in the mornings. We could watch the sunrise."

"I don't always get up *that* early," Lisa laughed.

"We could snuggle *and* watch the sunrise." Tom gently pulled Lisa closer and kissed her softly, sweetly on the lips. "And other things."

Lisa blushed and ducked her head. "I even sketched a picture of you," she said, lifting her head.

"Really?" Tom asked.

"Yes, I'll have to show it to you sometime." Lisa smiled. "Maybe I'll paint it when we get back."

Tom's heart sped up. He didn't want his picture painted. He didn't want to sit still for a painting. "That's flattering, I-I guess." Well, if it was sitting with Lisa, maybe not so bad. But still. No. No way. "You don't have to do that," he hedged.

"We'll see." Lisa's voice lingered like she'd paint it anyway whether he liked it or not. She ducked her head again.

Tom frowned and felt stoic. He had a feeling he didn't have a choice.

They were already quite a way from the hotel. Tom stopped and set down the basket. He turned and lifted Lisa's head with his fingers under her chin. "Don't hide from me. I always want to see those beautiful ocean-blue eyes looking at me."

Lisa blushed a deeper red and tried again to duck her head, but his fingers blocked that movement, then Tom slowly moved his hand and tangled it in her soft hair and crashed his lips against hers. This kiss was long and deep and sexy. He dropped her hand that he was holding and moved it around to her back and skimmed just above her rear. Oh, he wanted to squeeze her bottom, but he was afraid that would be too much for her. At least for right now. "Is this far enough?" Tom asked. "Or do you want to go a little bit further?"

Lisa slowly looked back at the hotel, at the ocean, the stars that were beginning to come out, one at a time, then at Tom. "I think this is far enough. Let's sit here."

Tom spread out the blanket and helped Lisa sit down, then he joined her. He leaned back on his elbows and looked at the sky.

"It sure is pretty here," Lisa said.

Tom looked at Lisa. "Yes, you are beautiful." Her hair was like summer wheat spread over the blanket. Her blue eyes filled with a craving he wanted badly to fulfill. He cupped her face and made love to her mouth— licking her lips, teasing her tongue, making her squirm beneath him. Lisa was so responsive, so passionate, so perfect for him. Despite all she'd been through, Lisa maintained an air of innocence that was thoroughly charming.

Lisa was breathless, a blush stained her cheeks. "Tom, that's not what I meant."

"I know exactly what you mean." He leaned over and cupped her silky hair and pulled her toward him as they kissed deeply. He let go of her hair and put his hand on her back and pulled her toward him, flush. Lisa moaned. Tom pulled her closer, if that was possible, all without breaking the kiss. He leaned her on her back, with him halfway over her. He started kissing her neck. Lisa arched her neck to give him access, and she moaned again. He ran his hand up and down her side. He didn't dare touch her breast, not after last time. Although he wanted to. He waited. He could be a patient man.

"Tom," Lisa panted.

"Yes, Lisa?"

"Oh, Tom, please."

"Please what? You're going to have to be specific. Talk to me. Tell me what you want, gorgeous," Tom panted.

"Touch me, please."

"Where, Lisa? Where shall I touch you? I'm already touching you here." He ran his hand along her side up from her hip to her shoulder.

"Tom, you're teasing me," Lisa laughed breathlessly.

"Yes, I want to tease you always, sweetheart," he breathed in her ear.

"And I'm touching you here…" He ran his fingers through her silky hair and massaged her scalp. "And I'm touching you here." He ran a finger down her face and cupped her cheek, then he kissed the other cheek.

"Oh, Tom, you know where," Lisa breathed.

"Yes, Lisa, but I want you to talk to me. Tell me exactly what you want, baby doll."

"Oh, Tom, touch my breasts."

Tom smiled slowly, his eyes softening. "Gladly, sweetheart. Thought you'd never ask."

CHAPTER 20

The next morning, the tenth day, the group went to the Top of the World in Koke'e State Park.

After they boarded the van, Pika started his information as he drove. "This park is squeezed between the signature peaks of the Na Pali coast and the bizarre wonder that is Waimea Canyon. This canyon is also known as the Grand Canyon of the Pacific. Koke'e State Park offers the most stunning land-based views in Kauai."

"Imagine. There's a Grand Canyon in Kauai!" Emma interrupted.

Pika paused, then continued, "The park covers a vast expanse of high-elevation terrain and is home to delicate ecosystems of endemic plants and animals."

Tom pointed for Lisa to look at the beautiful, leafy green area.

"The island of Niihau is only a short distance west of Kauai at that point where we are," Pika pointed out. "It can be clearly seen from the highway."

"Oooh! Look at that!" Emma squealed.

"For the best seat in the house," Pika continued, "tourists are encouraged to hike the incredible Awa'awapuhi Trail. Each person can treat themselves to amphitheater views."

"Oh! How pretty!" Olive sighed.

"It is now time to admire the Grand Canyon of the Pacific," Pika informed the group after they sat there a while. They continued on down the highway. The van made a turn, and words could not describe the beauty and grandeur of Waimea Canyon known as the Grand Canyon of the Pacific.

"It is hard to believe such a place exists on Earth," Pika spoke up. "Let alone on a small tropical island like Kauai."

Each person in the group gasped.

"When was the canyon formed?" Bill asked.

"The canyon was formed when Kauai's massive shield volcano collapsed and water took over to do the rest of the fine-tuning," Pika answered. "Dissected by the Waimea River, the canyon runs for over ten miles from north to south and is as deep as thirty-five hundred feet. It has dozens of incredible scenic overlooks."

"*Waimea* is Hawaiian for reddish water," Pika informed the group. "This is a reference to the erosion of the canyon's red soil. The canyon was formed by a deep incision of the Waimea River arising from the extreme rainfall on the island's central peak, Mount Wai'ale'ale, among the wettest places on earth.

Like the other Hawaiian Islands, Kauai is the top of an enormous volcano rising from the ocean floor. With lava flows dated to about five million years ago, Kauai is the oldest of the large Hawaiian Islands. Roughly four million years ago, while Kauai was still erupting almost continuously, a portion of the island collapsed. This collapse formed a depression which then filled with lava flows."This was more of a driving and sight-seeing day.

***

That night, Tom sidled up to Lisa and asked, "Want to go for a walk?"

"Mmm, maybe," Lisa answered.

"Maybe we can find another jeep buried in the sand," he suggested, wiggling his eyebrows.

Lisa laughed. There it was again, that beautiful tinkling sound of hers. He wanted to listen to her forever. "Of course, there is. They always bury jeeps in the sand so people can sit there and snuggle," she answered.

Damn, this girl had no idea how sexy she was. Everything about her was amazing. From her beautiful body, blue eyes, and blonde hair, to the way she helped everyone out, no questions asked. Tom's heart beat wildly, adrenaline coursing through him as he stepped closer.

"We can bring a blanket from the hotel and sit on it when we find a perfect spot," Tom said. "Like we did last night."

"What time shall we go then?" Lisa asked.

"Let's go after dinner."

"Okay."

After dinner, again, Tom and Lisa left the others and walked to the concierge's desk and picked up a basket, blanket, drinks, and started out onto the beautiful windswept beach. This time, they also included some fresh fruit.

Lisa and Tom walked on the beach, hand in hand. Tom was carrying the basket in one hand and holding Lisa's hand in the other. They arrived at the same spot as last night and spread out the blanket. Lisa sat down and Tom sat beside her.

As they sat down, Lisa pulled out some of the strawberries.

"How can you eat? We just ate back there," Tom teased.

"I need something sweet, yet not too sweet. Like a strawberry," Lisa laughed. She took a bite of the strawberry, her lips lingering around the ripe fruit. She closed her eyes and emitted a little moan that sounded all-too-familiar after their time together.

Tom swallowed hard and shifted in his seat.

When she opened her eyes, she seemed surprised to find him staring at her. She passed him the bowl of strawberries.

"Would you like some?" she asked, her eyes wide and innocent.

He cleared his throat. "No, thank you."

She was an enchantress. Completely without guile and yet with the power to render him speechless, helpless to do anything but want her. As he watched her take another strawberry, lift it to her full lips, he couldn't help thinking there were far more dangerous things in store for him. What was more dangerous than losing the woman who made him feel like he was breathing for the first time since he was a child? He reached over and captured her cheek with his hand and pulled her toward him in an erotic gesture and kissed her softly.

"Oh, Tom," Lisa breathed.

"Yes?"

"You are so sweet," she breathed.

"You're beautiful," he said, as he kissed her again.

"Tom, you're sweeping me off my feet," Lisa exhaled. "I don't know what to make of all of it."

"Believe it," Tom said. "It's real."

Lisa laid back on the blanket. Tom followed her down and started kissing her neck. He licked her collarbone, and Lisa arched her back, her breasts pressing up into his chest. He moved his other hand over to her tight T-shirt and started rubbing her breast. Lisa moaned. Tom squeezed her breast. Lisa moaned again and pushed her breast up into his hand. She wiggled beneath him. Tom so wanted to go farther with her, but he knew she would only go so far. At least for now. It was so hard to wait.

Tom moved his hand off her breast and moved it under her T-shirt. There, he felt her soft and sweet skin. Lisa sighed. He moved his big hand up to Lisa's bra underneath it and rubbed the underside of her breast. Lisa tried to squeeze her legs together, but he put his leg between hers, and she squeezed his leg. She moaned again. Tom pressed his body down on hers. She wiggled underneath him. He knew he had played with her breasts before, but Lisa was sometimes skitterish as a wild kitten. So he knew he had to go slow. Tom rubbed the underside of her breast again and moved up and caressed her breast, running his thumb lightly over Lisa's nipple.

"Oh, Tom," Lisa breathed. "Harder. Squeeze harder."

"Oh, yes, sweetheart." Tom was breathless too. He started his kisses back up her neck and licked Lisa's earlobe, then he pulled it lightly into his mouth and sucked.

Lisa squirmed underneath him. Tom smiled. He may not get anything tonight or anytime soon, but if she continued to like his ministrations, at some point, she would want to go further. And he wanted to be the one who took her there. And be there forever.

Tom pushed up her bra and T-shirt and exposed Lisa's breast to the outside air, caressing it all the while. She continued to wiggle underneath him.

No complaints here.

He squeezed her nipple with his fingers lightly, and Lisa moaned. He moved over and licked her nipple. Lisa sighed and squeezed his leg more. He leaned over and put his mouth over her breast and licked her nipple and grazed it with his teeth. Lisa's hips bucked up. Tom pressed his hips down at the same time. He wanted her to feel his erection and how bad he wanted her. He wasn't sure if this was going to work or backfire.

Lisa continued to move under him, so he moved his other hand under her T-shirt and her bra and caressed her nipple while he kissed this one, then he moved over and started kissing the other nipple, biting down softly.

"Oh, Tom," Lisa breathed. "Please."

"Please what, Lisa?" Tom asked around a mouthful of nipple and licked again, softly biting it.

"Oh, Tom, please. Oh please," Lisa begged, raring back.

"What do you want, sweetheart?" he asked softly, still licking and biting, alternating between softly and ramping it up by getting a little harder each time.

"Oh, Tom, please touch me."

"Where, Lisa?"

"Oh, Tom, you are such a tease," Lisa laughed. "Touch me down there. Please."

"Gladly, sweetheart."

"Oh, Tom…"

CHAPTER 21

The next day, the eleventh day, Tom, Lisa, and the rest of the group dressed to go swimming and snorkeling at Tunnels Beach. As the van headed toward Tunnels Beach, Lisa saw none of the scenery. Her mind was replaying the evening before with Tom.

As he kissed and fondled her, she smelled his wonderful cedar and woodsy spice cologne wrapping around her. She was thrilled at the unexpected sensations that fired through her. Without thought, she arched her back, pushing her farther into his palms. His thumbs traced a circle around her nipples, then flicked over the hardness, causing her to moan, then he looked Lisa in the eye and slowly pushed up her T-shirt till he got to her bra.

She had a pretty peach tone bra on. It was made of lace with a little tiny bow in the center and almost see-through. The straps were silky and smooth, and when she had tried it on, she instantly fell in love with it

Tom gently pushed the strap off her shoulder and the cup off her breast, then he licked her breast. Lisa bucked up, pushing her breast further into his mouth. He circled her nipple with his tongue. She moaned. He lightly nipped her nipple. She jumped up higher and moaned at the same time.

"Oh, Tom, that feels so good."

Then Tom moved the strap on the other shoulder and lowered the bra cup. He lavished the same treatment to the other breast as before. And he played with her down there. He put his big hand in her panties and his finger in her center. It felt so good. Lisa thought she had gone to heaven. She could hardly breathe even now at the memory.

But he went no further nor teased her into going further. After a long while, he looked into her eyes and smiled, then he kissed her. A long, slow hot kiss. And that was it. They stood up and went back to the hotel. She sure wanted more. Just not sure what more was. She still couldn't believe it. She'd thought all guys wanted one thing only, but Tom was turning out to be something else. Someone else. She was tickled about that. She did want more, just not yet.

"A penny for your thoughts?" Tom bumped her shoulder as he asked his question.

Lisa giggled and blushed bright red. "I don't think that you'd be interested in my thoughts," she stammered.

"I'm interested in everything about you." Tom smiled.

She flushed and ducked her head, partly because of what she had been remembering and hoping for and partly because Tom made her feel wanted and beautiful.

Tom reached over and picked up her chin with his fingers. "Don't hide from me," he said gently. "I always want to see your beautiful blue eyes looking right back at me." He leaned down and gently brushed his lips over hers. "Hear me?" he whispered.

Lisa nodded at the command.

"Good."

The van pulled up to Kauai's best beach, Makua Beach, better known as Tunnels Beach.

"This beach is as pretty as they come," Pika declared.

"Let's see what this is all about," Tom declared, lacing his fingers with Lisa's and pulling her down the aisle and off the van.

Tom and Lisa walked out onto a white sand beach in Makaha Beach Park with crystal clear waters and the pyramid-shaped Makana Mountain, better known as Bali Hai, looming in the background.

"We could easily spend the entire day here, swimming and snorkeling in Tunnels Beach," Emma declared.

"But we only have half a day here, then we go somewhere else. I forgot where," Sophia said.

"Why is it called Tunnels Beach?" Olive asked, changing the subject.

"The area is riddled with underground caves," Pika answered. "A few of them you can check out for yourself on the scenic coastal drive en route to Bali Hai."

"Bali Hai?" Emma squeaked. "Isn't that from *South Pacific*?"

"I will tell you all about Bali Hai when we get back in the van," Pika said, smiling.

"Well, let's go!" Emma encouraged the others, waving her arms to round up the group.

"Let's go swimming and snorkeling first!" Sophia looked at Emma pointedly.

"Then let's go swimming and snorkeling first!" Emma said.

"Let's pair up! We've been snorkeling before," Olive said as the group walked across the beach and into the water. Lisa and Tom walked hand in hand till the beach dropped off and they were able to snorkel easily. Lisa pointed at a blue fish swimming by, then they saw a sea turtle paddling along. The water was so clear, they could see all the way to the bottom of the bay.

They swam and snorkeled for about an hour and played on the beach for another hour, then they got out and dried off and had a picnic lunch. The girls changed back into their dry clothes on the other side of the van.

They finally got into the van and continued on the route to Bali Hai.

Everything was wonderful, yet Emma was quite frustrated at the length of time it took to finish looking at Tunnels Beach and then the time it took to get to Bali Hai.

"What's taking so long?" she asked.

"Bali Hai is a show tune from the 1949 Rodgers and Hammerstein musical *South Pacific*," Pika started his spiel. "The name refers to a mystical island, visible on the horizon but not reachable. It was originally inspired by the sight of the real island Ambaae from neighboring *Espiritu Santo* in Vanuatu, where author James Michener was stationed during World War II."

"Wow! That long ago!" Sophia exclaimed.

"Yes," Pika continued. "Michener referred to the island in his book *Tales of the South Pacific*, which is the basis for the musical *South Pacific*. The author used the tranquil, hazy image of the smoothly sloping island on the horizon to represent a not-so-distant-but-always-unattainable place of innocence and happiness. This is where the longing nature of the song comes from."

"There's so much history in these islands," Lisa mused. "I'm so glad you decided to come here, Olive."

She nodded and smiled. "Me too."

***

The next day, the twelfth day, the van took the group to the Green Foliage Helicopter tours. The four-passenger helicopter tour flew two copters to take the group to the majestic mountains, majestic sea caves, awesome waterfalls, and emerald green vistas. Many parts of Kauai are inaccessible, and the best way to see the breadth and majesty of Kauai was by air. Waimea Canyon, the Grand Canyon of the Pacific, was truly a spectacular sight from the air.

"Kauai's lush tropical setting features beautiful rainforests," the pilot said. "These breathtaking ocean-side cliffs and sparkling sand beaches are in stark contrast to Kauai's lushness. Thousands of years of volcanic activity, earthquakes, and erosion have created a dramatic variation in the landscape. The Waimea Canyon tour featured The Grand Canyon of the Pacific and offers one of the best views of the remote western coast of Kauai."

Emma squealed as the helicopter swung and flew dips and swooped over the awe-inspiring canyon. Waterfalls plunged from distant valleys. Azure blue skies, glowing red rocks, and brilliant green foliage combined for a study in color and contrast. The canyon rim was home to unique native tree ferns and koa forests with temperatures noticeably cooler than at sea level.

Historical and cultural sports provided a touch of romance to the tour. There were the remains of the early nineteenth-century Russian Fort, Fort Elizabeth, and Old Koloa Town, and old plantation town now known for the shopping and dining. They drove through the famous Koloa Tree Tunnel and stopped to visit the Spouting Horn—an ocean blowhole that also made a roaring sound reminiscent of a raging dragon.

On the eastern side of the island, they drove past the now-defunct Coco Palms resort grounds and up to the Opeakaa Falls overlook where a short walk led them to a view down into the Waiua River Valley. The historic waterway, which was Hawaii's only navigable river, ends at Fern Grotto—one of Kauai's signature attractions. Fern Grotto is only accessible by boat and provided sightseers an up-close view of the fern-lined cave and nearby waterfall. Local musicians and hula dancers entertained with songs and dance of old Hawaii while onboard the boat, and in the romantic setting of the Fern Grotto.

Later that afternoon, the group ziplined. Kauai zipline was the longest on the Kingston Ranch Adventures course. Lisa and Tom and the rest of the group harnessed up and climbed into the ranch's twelve-passenger ATV for a short ride to the trailhead. It was big enough to hold the eight-buddy moon group and four additional travelers. They clipped in and soared like birds over breathtaking valleys and streams as they embarked on a series of nine different crossings. Lisa walked through the treetops and over a waterfall on a suspension bridge that gave new meaning to the term suspension. She trembled when it swung back and forth. After a series of zips and walks, she arrived at a hidden treasure—an idyllic waterfall and swimming hole where the water was deep enough for Bill and Noah to jump from the surrounding rocks.

They swam around the pool, jumped off again and again. Emma and Sophia floated on inner tubes. Lisa, Tom, Olive, and Mason relaxed in hammocks while the guides prepared their picnic lunch.

That night, after getting back and changing clothes, the group went to a buffet luau dinner—the Tahitian Dancing in Luau Kalamaku. This award-winning dance in Kauai was currently considered to have the best Polynesian dance show of all island luaus. To the beating sounds of traditional drums, dozens of dancers told the story of a pair of Tahitian lovers separated as one departs on the long voyage to the Virgin Islands of Hawaii. Will they reunite in paradise? Will they survive the fury of the gods and rival chiefs? The group watched to find out. When the luau was over, Tom grabbed Lisa's hand and they stopped by the concierge's desk for a basket, blanket, drinks, and some fruit and went for a walk along the beautiful sunsetting beach.

They arrived at a spot and spread out the blanket, and Tom set down the basket. While Lisa stooped to straighten out the corner, he stepped behind her, then he pulled her against him. Lifting her hair, he touched his lips to her neck. She sighed as a shiver ran up her spine, her nipples turned hard. Tom snaked a hand around her stomach and up under her T-shirt. She leaned back against him, dropping her head back against his shoulder. He moved his hand up to her breast and up under her bra and caressed her nipple. Lisa moaned and stirred against him. His other hand meandered down to her center and rubbed her through her blue jean shorts. She about came undone. He held her tight against his body. She would have fallen if he hadn't. He rubbed her nipple back and forth in time with his other hand at her center. With his lips nibbling on her neck, Lisa could hardly breathe. It felt so good, she didn't want it to stop.

He moved his hand away from her center. She whimpered at the loss, then he moved in under her shorts, onto her skin, and down her body to her center again and slipped his finger into her.

"You are so wet for me," Tom said.

Lisa could only moan.

Tom hugged her tighter against his erection nestled between her buttocks."Oh, Tom," Lisa moaned. "What are we going to do?"

"I know what I want to do," he mumbled. "But you're not ready."

Lisa stirred in his arms. "What do you mean?" she asked.

"Oh, your body's ready. Your body wants what I can give you," Tom crooned.

"But?" Lisa asked, confused.

"But your mind is not quite there," he said. "Your emotions are not ready either."

Lisa's hip bucked against his fingers.

He pressed his fingers down harder.

She arched her back.

He rubbed her center harder.

She gasped and bent over and would have fallen if Tom hadn't held her tight. She shook with tremors all over her body.

"Oh god. What was that?" Lisa asked breathlessly. "It felt so good."

Tom just smiled and pulled her close.

CHAPTER 22

On the thirteenth day, they went hiking along the Mahaulepu Heritage Coastal Trail. It was nice to know there was one trail where the group of buddy-mooners might have nature all to themselves, especially on an island so frequented by visitors.

"You will have stunning views of the south shore," Pika told the group before they took off. "This coastal trail runs along the rugged coastline between Shipwreck and the Ha'ula beaches."

Along the way, they passed hidden coves protected by sharp limestone pinnacles. There were ancient Hawaiian stone structures, and schools of sea turtles came up for air in the pool of water they passed.

Around one of the bends, Tom pulled Lisa's hand to get her attention. When they stopped, he put the other one around her neck, under her hair, and gently pulled her close as their lips brushed together. Lisa's fingers came up around his neck. He put his arm around the small of her back and caressed her bottom, softly squeezing and pulling her closer.

Lisa moaned.

"Oh, Lisa. What are you doing to me?" he whispered in her ear. "I'm falling for you. I've never felt this way before. Please tell me you feel the same."

"Tom, of course. I'm falling for you too," Lisa breathed.

"Good. I couldn't stand it if you didn't," he whispered, pulling her closer.

He pulled her off the main trail and into the brush off to the side. They walked through the thick brush over their heads—not a trail—for quite a ways. They broke through and came to a small clearing.

"Ah, my lady, your castle awaits!" Tom exclaimed and swept his arm toward the clearing. Lisa tipped her head back and laughed.

"Thank you, Sir Knight."

Tom pulled her close and kissed her deeply. His hands roamed her back, up and down. They sank down onto the carpet of moss, Tom half-lying over Lisa. His fingers traced her knuckles as he pulled her fingers up and kissed them. His hand left hers and traced her face. The air around her smelled like lilacs. The hair on his arms rose. He was enjoying the beauty of this gorgeous, sweet, and kind woman. He stared into her clear blue eyes. She reached out and touched his arms. Electric bolts shot through him. The hum in his veins begged for her. Her hair was like silk as he ran his rough fingers through it to cradle her head.

A smile grew across her face.

His mouth brushed against hers. He wanted to kiss her forever.

Forever? Where did that come from?

Tom realized he wasn't panicking. Maybe forever was not so bad.

"I never met anyone I was serious about when I was looking," Tom said.

"I always assumed I'd have what my parents have," she said. "My dad is a stable guy who never gets upset about anything. My brothers are the same way. Laidback."

Am I stable enough? Tom wondered.

She continued as if she hadn't said anything impactful. "I always assumed I'd find a no-drama type of guy to settle down with."

The air around him crackled and he couldn't breathe, but at no point in his life did anyone think him rash.

He lifted his chin and asked, "Am I dramatic?"

"I don't know you well enough to say yet," she answered.

The kisses hadn't registered as important enough. He'd have to test that. "Your blue eyes haunt my dreams," Tom whispered into Lisa's ear. "Your kiss is embedded on my lips." He kissed her like she was the most important person in his life. "You being here is the most important part of all this, and I don't want to lose what we have."

"Tom! Lisa! Where do you think they went?" they could hear their friends calling from the trail.

Lisa's eyes widened. "Should we answer?"

"Not yet," Tom answered. "We've still got plenty of time."

They started kissing again. Tom kissed her neck and down to her collarbone. Her pulse was fluttering at her neck.

He loved the look of that little flutter. He reached up and nipped her ear, making Lisa wiggle under him. He wanted to do so much more, go so much further. Would she let him? Or would she throw up a wall and keep him at arms-length? And if she did, could he coach her back to him? He'd never worried about that before, but he'd never been with someone so fragile before, or so inexperienced, so innocent.He rested his head on his palms and stared at Lisa. She was so beautiful and didn't seem to know it, even when he said it.

"What'cha looking at?" Lisa asked.

"You."

"Why?"

"Because I love looking at your luscious face."

Lisa blushed and lowered her eyes.

"Don't look away from me, please, sweetheart. I love looking at those beautiful crystal blue eyes."

She looked at him, her mouth partially agape. He thought she looked so sexy that way. He brushed his thumb over her lower lip, and she looked up at him. He pulled her down and kissed her—a slow, soft kiss. It didn't take long for it to morph into a deep kiss, their tongues doing a sexy dance. He reached his hand up and cupped her cheek, moving his thumb in slow circles. After a while, he moved his hand down slowly and cupped her breast. Lisa moaned. He just deepened the kiss and started kneading her breast through her blouse, running his thumb over her nipple.

Lisa groaned and pushed her breast into his hand.

He squeezed. He moved his hand around her back and pulled Lisa close. He wanted to keep her close always, protect her in all ways.

Protect her? From what? Anything and everything. Him? Just keep her close.

He buried his face in her hair at her neck. She smelled so good. *Lilac?* He was beginning to love that scent.

"I could stay here forever." Lisa's stomach growled. "Do you think anyone would miss us? Should we go back now?" Lisa asked.

"Let's not go back just yet. Let's snuggle some more," Tom answered. "What time is it? I'm hungry," she asked.

Tom pulled out his phone. "It's a little after noon. You really want to go in and find them?"

"I'm hungry. Pika's got our lunch."

"Oh, right. Let's go."

"How do we get out of here?" Lisa asked.

"O-oh," Tom stammered. He'd been in such a hurry to get her away from the others that he forgot to plan a way back out. "It wasn't that far? Was it?"

"I was following you, Tom. I wasn't paying attention either."

He looked up. The sun was straight up. It was noon. That wouldn't help. He looked around the foliage on the ground. Nothing looked trampled. *Which way had they come in?* He looked at the ground where they had laid. Which way were their feet turned? *Okay!*

"This way." Tom grabbed Lisa's hand, and they started pushing through the undergrowth for what seemed like an hour. *Was it getting thicker?* It hadn't taken them that long to get there. It shouldn't take that long to get back. Tom pulled out his phone. It was 1:30PM. *An hour and a half!* Tom was worried now, but he couldn't let Lisa know. He pulled up his GPS on his phone. Maybe that would work.

"What's wrong, Tom?" Lisa asked. She laid her hand on his arm.

"Nothing. Thought I'd try my GPS for a while."

"It's 1:30 already! No wonder I'm so hungry!"

"We'll find something to eat."

"What?" Lisa asked. "Are you some wilderness guru? Do you know which leaves to eat and which are poisonous? I don't! Do you?"

"Lisa, let me see if I can get this GPS working right."

"What's GPS gonna do?"

"Well, if the trail is on the GPS, then we'll see where we are and go in that direction."

After a time, Lisa asked, "Is it working?"

"No," Tom sighed deeply. "It won't go to that detail. It only goes to the roads. It does show where we are, but I'm not sure how to get to the road from here."

Tom was really getting worried. He didn't know what to do. He was a city boy, not a wilderness expert. What if they didn't find their way back before dark? What then? What would they eat? Where would they sleep? For all he knew, they could just be feet from the path and not know it. He was so out of his element.

"Sorry, I panicked," Lisa said. "I might remember some things about wilderness stuff. I was in the Girl Scouts in high school for a time. I dropped out as a junior, so I didn't finish, but I got some training."

"Did you learn about what leaves to eat and what to leave alone?" Tom asked, smirking a little.

"I did, but that was in North America. Here on the islands, I imagine that's different. I might remember how to make fire from sticks, but I need a clearing. I wouldn't want to set this brush on fire."

They were standing in a bunch of brush high over their heads.

"Then we need to get moving," he said.

"But which direction?" she asked.

"This way," Tom said, pointing. "We didn't get to the Makauwahi Cave, so we go in the opposite direction."

"How can we tell what is the opposite direction?"

"Well, we will once we get on the path."

"We're in all this brush," Lisa pointed out.

"I just don't want to run parallel to the path we were on while we're in the brush," Tom answered.

"Tom, where is the path?"

"I don't know," he sighed, then he rallied. "Let's go this way."

"Okay…"

They trampled *that* direction, not knowing if it was right or not for another hour. Tom had turned off his phone to preserve the battery but turned it back on to check the time. They stumbled out of the brush and onto bare rock. Now, where were they? It was getting dusk. "Why haven't you called them yet?" Lisa asked.

"I thought we'd find the trail before now."

"Well?"

'Okay. Okay." Tom started dialing Mason. No answer. He dialed Noah, no answer, so he dialed Bill. "Bill! You answered!"

"Tom? Where are you guys?"

"Uh… we're lost."

"Why are you lost, Tom?" Bill asked. Bill sounded way too calm.

"We stepped off the path."

"Why did you do that, Tom?" Bill asked in that calm voice.

"Uh… we went exploring," Tom hedged.

"Yeah, right. What did you explore? Never mind," Bill chuckled. "How do we find you?"

"If I knew that, we'd be home by now."

"Let's see if we can track your cell phone." Bill covered his phone receiver to speak to someone else. "My gosh! How did you get that far off the trail?"

"I don't know," Tom answered."Hold on."

After a few minutes, Bill came back. "I just spoke to the park ranger. He says it's too late to come to get you now. Stay where you are and we'll come to get you tomorrow morning. Wait a minute, Tom!" In a few moments, Bill came back on. "Okay, Tom, turn off your phone so you can preserve your battery and turn it back on in the morning at 6AM so we can find you. And do *not* move far from where you are. We want to find you tomorrow."Tom hung up.

"What do we do now?" Lisa asked with a slight tremble.

Tom tried to sound reassuring as he told her what Bill had said. They would have to stay there until morning.

They looked around at their soundings—bush on one side and rock on the other.Lisa sat down on the rock. "I can gather sticks from the brush to make a fire, but I really don't want to sleep out in the open on a rock."

Just then, her stomach growled.

"Or sitting on the beach on a blanket." She smiled, sensing his sorrow. "I wanted to lag behind with you too. It's just as much my fault that we're lost."

For a moment, Tom beheld the beauty and graciousness of the woman who had captured his heart. "Well…" he replied quickly, pretending to make light of the dangerous situation. "We can still make out."

"Tom…"

'We can't?" She pursed her lips, playfully feigning a rebuff.

Suddenly, all his anxieties disappeared. When he was with Lisa, he felt like he could endure anything.

"C'mere, baby," he said, bending down and pulling on her hands. He pulled her up to standing from where she had been sitting. All of a sudden, she burst into tears. "Shh, just get it all out."

After a while, she blubbered, "I'm too big to cry over this." *Sniff.* "We'll get picked up." *Sniff, sniff.* "In the morning."

"Yes, we will. It's okay to cry. When you're done, how about if you go hunt for some sticks, and I'll look for a better place for us to settle down for the night."

"I do have my phone."

"And why didn't you call either?" Tom asked, chuckling.

"I thought you knew what you were doing."

"Well, now we know I didn't," Tom admitted

"We didn't get lost on purpose?" Lisa asked.

"No!" Tom exclaimed. "I thought we could get ourselves back out of there. Easily. Obviously, I was wrong."

Lisa smiled. "Yeah," she said softly.

Tom looked a little chagrinned. Lisa reached over and touched his arm. He pulled her over and gave her a kiss. She turned her head, and he deepened the kiss. He reached his hand down and pulled her closer, flush to his body. Lisa moaned. He started kissing her neck.

"Tom…" He could hear her breath.

"Yes, baby?" He continued to kiss her neck, smelling her lilac perfume.

"Shouldn't we be getting ready before it gets dark?"

He nipped her ear and inhaled, "I suppose so." He kissed her again, softly, slowly, and pulled her tighter.

"Tom…" Lisa whispered against his lips, pushing him back.

"Okay… let's go," he said, breathing hard.

"Okay. I'll go this way and gather twigs and brush," she said.

"Yes, and I'll go this way and see what's in that direction."

"Now don't you get lost, dear," she teased.

He reached over, grabbed her around the waist, and kissed her hard. "Okay, I won't."

Lisa laughed and started into the brush. She walked along the edge of the rockface.

Tom started in the opposite direction. He walked quite a way and then saw it. A cave. He bent over and called into the cave. How far did it go? He went exploring. Oh, it wasn't too deep, but he had to bend over to get to the back. He stepped off the distance from the back to the mouth of the cave and realized that it was big enough to sleep at the back and have a fire at the front. He hurried back to Lisa.

"Whoa! That's a lot of brush and sticks," he said as he approached her pile of twigs and brush.

"I thought we might want to sleep on something. And I didn't know how long it would take to burn all night. Assuming we let it burn all night," Lisa said.

"Well, it may be a good thing I found a cave, just the right size to sleep in and have a fire at the mouth of it."

"A cave?"

"Yes, let's gather up this and move it there. Come on." Tom bent over and gathered as much as he could carry and walked over to the cave. He dumped the brush in the back. Lisa had followed him with most of the sticks and put those in the front of the cave. They went back for a second and third load.

"Now, is this soft enough to sleep on?" Tom asked Lisa.

"Some of the brush needs to be used for the fire starter, but after that, the sticks should be enough. If I got enough to last all night," she said.

"Let's check it out. Lie down," Tom insisted.

Lisa huffed but laid down on the brush. "It's a little sticky, but it's okay."

"A little sticky?"

"Yes, you know, the sticks in the brush poke into you." Lisa smiled.

"Lisa…"

Lisa laughed and leaned up on her elbow.

Tom leaned down and sat beside her. "You think you're funny, don't you?"

"Of course." She smiled up at him.

"You do, do you?" Then he started to tickle her.

Lisa giggled and wiggled around and tried to get out of his reach, then they paused, looking deep into each other's eyes, and Tom kissed her. Then he intensified the kiss. He moved his hand down her back and slightly rubbed her bottom, then he started nibbling on her neck.

"Tom…" Lisa breathed. "Shouldn't I start the fire?"

He nipped her ear. "I'll do it." Tom got up and walked over to the sticks. He started rubbing two sticks together with no luck. He kept trying for quite a while. "This is hard," he complained, frustrated.

Lisa got up and came over to sit beside him. "Want me to try?"

"Humph!" Tom snarled. "If you want to."

Lisa started rubbing two sticks together. Again and again. It took forever, but finally, a spark showed up. She grabbed some brush and put it on the spark. It caught on. She laid the sticks—two biggest on the bottom, two crosswise and built it up with sticks around it, added some more brush, and it started flaming.

"Now what?" Lisa asked Tom, looking up at him demurely.

"Well, I'm impressed!" he answered. He reached for her. "You really are a girl scout, Wilderness woman."

Just then, Lisa's stomach growled. She sighed as she sat down beside him.

"I'm sorry I don't have anything for you to eat, sweetie," Tom said.

"I don't have anything for you to eat either." Lisa smiled.

"Are you saying I'm chauvinistic?"

"Of course not." Lisa smiled. "Maybe a little condescending."

"And here I thought I was being a knight in shining armor," Tom laughed. He pushed a curl of her hair behind her ear and brought his finger down her ear, chin, and neck. He leaned down and kissed her closed eyes.

"Of course you are," she giggled. "You can be my knight in shining armor."

Tom cupped her cheek and stared into her eyes. "Since we don't have anything to eat, we've got nothing else to do other than sleep." He smiled.

Lisa smiled shyly, trying to duck her head and dropping her eyes.

"Look at me, sweetheart," Tom whispered. "Open those beautiful blue eyes." He stretched out the word beautiful. "I know you're gorgeous and I want to look at you. I want you to look back at me."

Lisa looked up, blushing bright red.

"You know you're so stunning when you blush."

"Right," she said.

"No, really," he said. "That's what I love about you—your shyness and blushes," Tom said. "I'm just blown away by your looks and your personality. You're beautiful all over, inside and out."

"Thank you," she whispered.

He leaned over and kissed her, long and slow.

Lisa turned her head, and he escalated the kiss. She laid onto her back as Tom laid half on and half off her, rubbing his hand up and down her side. Her hand gripped his shirt. She moaned into his mouth.

He wanted to go so much further with her, but this was not the place to do it. He started stroking her breast. Their tongues danced erotically. His thumb flicked over her nipple.

She groaned.

Tom smiled against her lips.

"Oh, Lisa…" he whispered.

"Tom…"

Tom moved his big hand under her blouse and over her breast, caressing her nipple with his thumb.

Lisa moaned.

Tom leaned over and took her breast into his mouth, flicking his tongue over her nipple.

Lisa pushed her back into his mouth, giving him better access.

He snaked his other hand down and into her shorts and in her underwear… into her center.

Lisa wiggled against him.

One hand on her breast, his mouth on the other, and the other hand at her center. Tom licked her nipple, pressing it with his tongue.

"Harder. Press harder," Lisa breathed.

He caressed her center a little harder, flicked her nipple with his fingers a little harder, and grazed her other nipple with his teeth and pulled.

Lisa gasped, nearly doubling over, but she couldn't. Tom laid half on top of her.

"Oh, Tom," Lisa groaned. "That felt so good. Shouldn't we do something for you?"

"No, Lisa," he sighed. "It's probably a good idea to go to sleep right now."

"Oh…"

"Yes, here you lie on your side and face the fire and I'll lie right behind you." Tom wrapped his arm around her stomach, under her breast, cupping his fingers over her breast and pulling her close. He really wanted to do more but was reasonably sure she wasn't ready for the 'more' he wanted to do. He made himself behave.

"Tom…"

"Yes, Lisa?"

"I need to go… um…"

"Go where?"

"Out there." She smiled sheepishly, tilting her head toward the bushes.

"Oh," he laughed. "Allow me to escort you to the ladies' room. I'll stand by the front of the cave and look the other way, okay?"

"Okay."

Nervous, Lisa watched him the whole time. She would die with embarrassment if he peeked, yet Tom was a perfect gentleman, waiting until she cleared her throat before he turned around and helped her back to the cave. No longer worried about being lost in the middle of nowhere, Lisa lay down beside him.

CHAPTER 23

When Lisa rested next to him, Tom turned her on her back. He kissed her soundly, fiercely. "Oh, sweetheart," he whispered. Oh, he wanted to kiss her all night, make sweet love to her, bring her to orgasm dozens of times, but he had to behave. He also felt guilty for getting them lost.

"Uh, Tom…" She struggled to whisper back. "You sure we can't make you come tonight?"

He leaned over and kissed her mouth slowly, deliberately. He slowly touched his tongue to her lips and she opened her lips for him invitingly. Tom dove in. He licked her tongue with his tongue and the sides of her mouth. He was so hard, he could hardly stand it. Her moan nearly did him in. Their tongues danced in remembered joy, getting serious with every thrust. She lifted her arms to circle his neck and pulled him in close.

Tom moved from her mouth to her cheek, then her chin and neck. He sighed. He so wanted in her right now, but he knew it was her decision. Because of the rape. He hesitated. She pulled him closer. He licked her pulse where her neck met her shoulder, then he licked her collarbone.

Lisa groaned and pushed her pelvis up to his. He groaned himself into her mouth and ground up against her. Tom moved his hand and unbuttoned the top button of her shirt. Lisa pushed up into his hand. He smiled. She was so responsive.

How can anyone not know that?

Her hips wiggled against him. He groaned. He unbuttoned the next button and the next. When he had all the buttons undone, he slipped his hand inside and cupped her breast over her bra. She moaned. He reached in and pulled her breast out of her bra. Her heart was beating so fast, he could feel it matching his. He cupped her breast and leaned over and licked her nipple. She pushed it up into his hand. He leaned down and put his mouth on her breast and sucked it.

Tom leaned back and looked at her. The fire danced shadows over her sweet skin. He admired her figure. She was so firm. "Oh, sweetheart, you are so beautiful."

Lisa's eyes shot open, and she looked at him and smiled. "Really?" she asked, doubtful.

"Oh, yes!" he exclaimed and kissed her again. Hard. Then he kissed her breast and played his thumb over the other one.

Lisa moaned.

He stroked her hair, his hands gentle but sure.

"Please don't stop," Lisa begged.

"This?" he asked, running his hand up her side.

"Yes," she said. "That feels so good." Her eyes shut in a sigh, and she breathed in slowly.

Then he slowly ran his hand up and down her side, from her hips to the underside of her breast. When he reached her breast this time, he slowly reached over and rubbed her nipple. Lisa groaned. Tom felt like he was a horny teenage boy again. He felt like he was going to come any minute now.

All at once, she stiffened. Closing his eyes, Tom stopped. He tried to calm down. Tom had never loved a woman as much as he loved Lisa. Now, he fought to control the instinctive urges within him. He felt tortured. He opened his eyes and sighed. "Lisa, I think we'd better go to sleep."

"You think I'm not ready, don't you?" Lisa asked.

"You deserve to have your first time in a big beautiful bed. Soft linens. Pillows all around. A four-poster bed with soft fluffy sheets," he said, scanning the leaves, sticks, and dirt in the cave. "I want to worship you properly. Not take you just because I'm horny. I want to treat you like the princess you are! Like the queen you have become in my eyes."

Suddenly, Lisa was quiet and looked away.

Tom gently lifted her chin. "What's the matter, sweetheart?"

"I've already had my first time… in a car," Lisa sniffed.

"Not with me," Tom murmured. He reached over and ran his hands through her hair. He pulled a strand out and brought it to his lips and kissed it. He took a deep breath. "Lisa, tell me more about what happened. I want you to feel safe in my arms, that you can tell me anything. Just talk to me, sugar."

Lisa's voice trembled. "Grey was the hottest, most popular guy in high school. All of us girls had a crush on him. He was captain of the football team. Big, muscular, sexy, and smooth-taking. He could talk any of the teachers into letting him have an A, and the football coach thought the world of Grey too. He was a god. At least in our high school. Don't know what he was like in college, but I found that out later that he could do anything and get away with it. So I didn't go."

"Wow," Tom said. "You didn't go to college because he was there?

She lowered her head. "I couldn't tell anyone that he had raped—" she paused, "done something bad. No one would believe me," Lisa whispered. "He seemed to walk on water everywhere he went."

"Oh, Lisa."

"Tom, I was so flattered that someone like him actually asked me out," Lisa said. "He only dated the popular girls. I was just a quiet art student who kept to herself. I couldn't have been more surprised that day when he asked me to go to the movies with him."

"Did he try anything at the movies?" Tom asked.

"No. Not at the movies. We saw *The Avengers*. I don't remember which one now," Lisa recalled. "It was so action-packed that it could have been anyone sitting beside him. He didn't seem to notice me then."

"But after the movie?" Tom encouraged, carefully.

"Yeah, after the movie, we went to lover's lane outside of Grove. It was a construction site, just outside of town, and no one was there. He started telling me how pretty I was and how good my paintings were. He said he'd been watching me, noticing how quiet I was. It sounds like stalking to me now, but at the time, I was so proud that someone like Grey seemed interested in me—little ol' me. Nothing me."

Tom was livid. "Oh, sweet Lisa. You are not a nothing. You are beautiful and fun. I'll bet you were different than the girls he usually dated."

"He did say that," Lisa exclaimed. "And I was surprised because he dated everyone. He got around. A lot. So when he said he wanted to see why I was so different, so unique. Oh, Tom! I… I let my guard down, just enough, or I would have jumped out of that car sooner. I shouldn't have trusted him. I should have known better. That's why I believed it was my fault all this time," Lisa said sadly.

"Yeah, he found out you were different, all right! You wouldn't put up with his shenanigans. His crap. His waste of time. You *did* leave, Lisa."

"Not until it was over," she mumbled. "I had to walk a long way, then a police car picked me up. He saw my rumpled clothing and guessed immediately what happened, but I kept denying it, even as I cried. I denied it," Lisa said.

"What did the policeman do?" Tom asked.

"Oh, he took me to the police station. Another policeman found Grey and brought him in. He saw me and acted like we knew each other but had not been together that night. The police knew, but I was so frightened that I denied it was him," Lisa said.

"If the police knew, then he'd done it before," Tom said gently. "And they had caught him before or at least suspected him of it."

Tom couldn't believe it. He wanted to tear this guy limb from limb. Tom hated to imagine what Lisa went through, how she cried and screamed. He wondered how this guy could take advantage of such a beautiful, innocent young girl.

"I hadn't thought about that before," Lisa said, looking up at Tom. "I sure didn't think about it then," Lisa huffed. "I was so ashamed that I didn't want anyone to know about it, least of all a male policeman."

"Didn't they have any policewomen?" Tom asked, aghast.

"Well, yes. After I got into the room to take pictures of my torn clothing, bruises."

"Bruises?"

"Oh, yes. He hit me. He tried to control me while he raped me," Lisa said stoically. "I wouldn't stay still. But he did seem to like it that I struggled. That seemed to turn him on. So I quit struggling. Just let him do it." She looked up at Tom sadly. "He pinned my arms down up beside my body. I couldn't move."

"Oh, Lisa."

"Tom, I don't want to talk about it anymore."

"I'm right here," he assured her. "Sleep, darling."

Lisa turned over and faced the fire. Neither made any attempt to move apart. Tom held her as if she'd always slept in his arms. When he closed his eyes and his heartbeat slowed to a deep sleep, a single thought skipped through his mushy, dreamlike-filled brain—*We're good together*.

Mine.

CHAPTER 24

*L*isa had almost fallen into the abyss of sleep when the last thought drifted across her mind.

He called me darling.

When she woke up, Tom's hand was cupping her breast. Lisa remembered that as she closed her eyes last night, she had let the warmth of his voice settle over her nerves like a lullaby.

Now all she could think about was him calling her darling. Lisa wanted to lie on her back and let him have his way with her. She felt so confused. This was the fourteenth day of the trip. She couldn't make up her mind if she liked that or not. The fire was just coals now. The sky was light. Wondering what time it was, Lisa tried to figure out how to move out of Tom's embrace without waking him up. Instead, he pulled her closer. "Good morning, sweetheart," he whispered in her ear, then he tugged her over on her back and kissed her deeply, slowly. Even after being lost overnight, he still smelled of cedar and that woodsy cologne. He ran his hand down her side and caressed her hip, then he ran that same hand up her body and softly grabbed her breast. Lisa moaned into his mouth. He rubbed her nipple with his thumb. She was so turned on that she was ready to do anything he wanted. She hoped he'd rip off her clothes and take her right there, right then. And that scared her. Her lusty thoughts for him clouded her judgment. She rubbed the back of her neck and tried to cool down. Her stomach growled.

"Tom, I need to go to the restroom," Lisa whispered against his lips.

"Okay. Hurry back."

Tom kissed her hard and let her up.

After she came back, Tom said, "I turned on my phone. It's before six, and I don't know how long they will take to track us."

"Should we move back over by the brush?"

"Nah, they said don't go too far. And we're not too far from where we were."

"All right."

"We'll just snuggle on this bed we've got here for a while and wait for them to call," he said, pulling her close.

They lay back on the brush bed they had slept on and he nudged her onto her back. She wasn't sure anymore that she wanted to do this. It scared her because she really did want to snuggle and kiss and go further than that, but people were coming to find them. The time would have been last night, but Tom had insisted they sleep.

"Lisa, you are so wonderful." He ran his hand up and down her side, landing on her thigh, and he squeezed gently.

Lisa was so turned on that she almost came unglued. She wanted to be, but she didn't want to be. Lisa was so confused. When he tweaked her nipple, however, she did come undone.

"Tom…" she gasped and curled in. He held her tight as she had another orgasm.

"Lisa, are you okay?" he asked.

"Yes," she answered, still breathing hard.

"Wait… Lisa…" he panted. "What if we go sit by the coals?"

"You're right, Tom. You're right. Let's do that." Lisa got up and sat on the rock by the opening of the cave with her knees up. Tom sat beside her, cross-legged.

"Lisa…"

"Yes, Tom?"

"I'm sorry. I went too far," he said.

"No. Apparently, my body liked it." Lisa tried to smile. "But I guess I'm not ready for it mentally." She didn't think he went too far. If Tom hadn't been so understanding, she would have gone further.

"I don't want you to be mad at me," he said.

"I'm not."

"Then what is it?" He scooted closer to her.

Lisa hung her head.

Tom reached over and picked up her chin, turned her head with his fingers. "Look at me, sweetheart. Tell me."

"No." She lifted her head but kept her eyes down.

"Why not?"

"I'm embarrassed," she sighed.

"Don't be embarrassed around me. Tell me. I won't laugh. I promise."

She lifted her eyes and bit her lip. "You'll laugh."

"No, I won't," he assured.

She looked at him and sighed heavily. "Oh, all right. Every time you touch me like that, I want to, but I don't want to. Not yet. I think."

"You want to what?" Tom asked.

"You know," she whispered.

"No. Tell me, Lisa. Just what are you talking about?"

"You're mean, Tom! This is a game for you. You know what I'm talking about, and you just want to make me say it." Now she was angry with him. She didn't want to say *it*.

"Lisa, I want you to say it. I want you to be clear about what you want. That's not a game to me."

"But I'm not clear about anything!" she protested. She wanted to have sex, but she didn't. Confused, she didn't know how to explain it.

"Lisa…" he said, trying to put his arm around her, but she lifted her shoulder and scooted away.

"See? That's why I haven't pushed you because you're not ready."

"Will I ever be ready?" she wailed.

"Of course, you will. With the right guy, you will be." Now Tom hung his head. "Maybe I'm not him."

"Oh… I think… you could be." Lisa really wanted it to be him.

"Yeah?" Tom asked, looking up.

"Yeah," she answered. *At least I hope so*, she thought.

"C'mere, sweetheart." He scooted over closer to her.

She turned into him. He wrapped his arms around her. She snuggled into him.

"Lisa, I know it's early. It's only been days, less than two weeks, but I think I'm falling in love with you."

"Really?"

"Yeah, I really believe that," Tom said

"Me too. I-I t-think I'm falling in love with you too." Lisa couldn't believe what he'd said and that she actually answered.

Suddenly, Tom's phone rang. "Hello?"

He put it on speaker. It was Bill.

"So we've got you pinged. We know exactly where you are. Just stay put. The park rangers are coming on two four-wheelers and will take you out. You really are *off* the path," Bill teased. "Some exploring."

Tom held the phone with one hand and put his arm around Lisa and pulled her close. "Yes," he said. "We've had quite an exploring adventure." He kissed her quietly so Bill wouldn't hear.

"You still there?" Bill asked.

"Yeah, we're still here," Tom answered, still with his arm around Lisa. He pulled her closer.

"Well, you guys got quiet," Bill said.

"Well, we're still here," Tom insisted.

"I'm supposed to stay on the line until the four-wheelers show up. Just in case they're not the right ones."

"What do you mean not the right ones?"

"Oops. Maybe I wasn't supposed to say that part."

"You think there're bandits out here on four-wheelers? Like our rescuers?" Lisa squeaked.

"You have me on speakerphone? And she heard that?"

"Yep," Tom answered.

"Great. Just great!" Bill groaned.

"Is there some kind of code word I'm supposed to say to know it's the right guys?"

"No, they'll be in park ranger uniforms."

Lisa and Tom sat there for a while chatting with Bill about nothing and anything that came to mind.

Suddenly, they heard the roar of engines. The ATVs were arriving. Bill stayed on the line. They stood up.

Two ATVs roared by them, then they turned around and came back and pulled up. A Honda Pioneer 1000 EPS and Polaris RZR S 1000 EPS.

CHAPTER 25

The first thing Tom noticed was that they weren't wearing park ranger uniforms. Each rider pulled off his helmet.

Tom gulped and whispered into the phone to Bill, "These are not the park rangers. You should be able to hear since you're still on speakerphone."

"The rangers will be there any minute. Stay calm. Talk to them. Try to make friends with them."

"Okay," Tom answered.

As he sized-up the two men, however, Tom held on to his phone in shock.

"Well, well, well… what do we have here, Scratch?" the one with a snake tattoo on his neck said. "Looks like ripe pickings, boss," Scratch answered.

"Hello, gentlemen," Tom called. "How are you today?" Tom reached over and pulled Lisa close. He could feel her trembling.

"Maybe we could have some fun with our new friends," the boss answered.

The boss had so many tattoos that Tom immediately thought of him as tattoo guy.

"Maybe we could." Scratch smiled evilly.

Tom slipped the phone to Lisa and let go of her. "Stay behind me," he whispered, then he called out the ATV riders. "We have some park rangers coming up to help. Why don't you guys just move along."

"Oh, you do?" Scratch said. He looked at tattoo guy and asked, "Do you believe them?"

Scratch was skinny and wiry. Tattoo was heavy and tall, his bulk was all muscle, no fat. Tom could see that right away. He swallowed, scared to death. "Nah, I don't. I think they are making that up," Tattoo said. "Let's check them out." He lifted his leg and got off his ATV. So did Scratch.

Tom's experience was exercising, working out on weights, and Jiu-Jitsu. Jiu-Jitsu helped with balance, flexibility, and overall fitness. It included kickboxing and mixed martial arts. He had practiced fighting on the mat at the gym, but he'd never fought someone for real. Tom hoped he remembered his training, but he was still trying to appear calm.

"We don't have anything. We're just hikers about to move on. You don't have to check us out," Tom said.

While the men stared at Lisa, Tom wondered if he should crouch in fighting form or if that would just challenge them. He could sense Lisa's terror while Bill talked on the phone.

She was frozen stiff. Afraid to put it up to her ear, Lisa held the phone down by her side.

"What kind of jewelry do you have on you?" Tattoo asked, eyeing their necks and hands.

"We don't' have anything on us," Tom called. "The van driver has it all. Everything is on the van."

"Well, now, which is it?" Tattoo sneered. "Are you hikers or riding in a van?"

"The van dropped us off and will be here soon to pick us up," Tom answered.

"I thought you said the park rangers were coming," Scratch mocked.

"They're both coming," Tom added quickly, feeling like he had been caught in a lie. He was glad they were just talking… so far. Yet he couldn't help wonder what was taking the rangers so long to arrive.

"You don't mind if we check that out for ourselves, do you?" Scratch asked nastily, like he didn't mean it. "To see what you've got?"

"Yeah, I do," Tom snapped. "Well, we'll just have to persuade you." Tattoo smiled with a sneer, then he slowly pulled out a huge shredder knife and brandished it with excitement. "Does this change your mind, big brave man?"

"Just move along," Tom growled, his eyes in slits.

Tattoo and Scratch swaggered toward them.

Tom lifted his fists and crouched in a fighting stance. "Don't go into the cave," Tom whispered fiercely to Lisa. "They could trap you there."

Scared, Lisa's eyes got wide, and she moved behind Tom.

"Hey, little girlie, why don't you come over here and sit by me while those two big strong men fight it out?" Scratch called.

All of a sudden, he heard Lisa exhale with defiant stand. "No!" she shouted.

Surprised but also proud of her courage, Tom immediately felt strong and more powerful than ever before. "Awe, don't be like that." Scratch grinned then, laughing wickedly. He circled to Tom's left. He neared Lisa while Tattoo approached her from the other side.

She shook as Scratch gazed at her.

Tom could see her out of the corner of his eye.

"Hey, girlie. Look at me!" Scratch snickered.

"Leave her alone," Tom said vehemently.

Lisa trembled, but she narrowed her eyes in disgust.

"Don't look at me like that, little sweetie," Scratch mocked as if he was about to devour a steak.

Petrified, Lisa stared at his rotten teeth.

Tom wondered how to stall them until the park rangers showed up.

Tattoo began to make his move. As he approached, Lisa stepped closer behind Tom.

Tom knew that time was running out. They were trapped. The cave was behind them, and the ATVs were in front of them. There was no place to go.

Tattoo laughed as if he knew it too. Smiling, he waved the knife at Tom.

Tom's hands opened wide. He wanted to take down that knife.

Lisa glanced between the knife, Scratch, Tattoo, and Tom in panic.

Suddenly, Tattoo sliced his knife toward Tom's stomach, but Tom jumped away instinctively, Sure-footed, he managed to avoid hitting Lisa in the maneuver. Tom kept an eye on Lisa, who had stepped backward. In one swift motion, he reached down, grabbed one of the sticks from the campfire, and slung it at the knife. When the knife clattered across the rock floor, Tom lunged at Tattoo with the stick, hoping to pierce his unprotected belly.

Home run! Tom thought, standing up victoriously, amazed by his performance. Just then, however, Tattoo pivoted into a crouch that cracked the burned stick. He took advantage of Tom's momentary gloat. In a second, Tattoo rammed his fist into Tom's gut, sending him reeling to the ground, the breath burst from his lungs.

Tattoo spun around with a powerful roundhouse kick that knocked the stick from Tom's hand. As it thudded away, breaking into pieces, Tom realized that Tattoo's martial arts skills equaled his own.

I'm not letting my guard down again, he thought.

Yet fighting a giant came with advantages. Tom had a lower center of gravity, so it was harder for the big lug to knock him off balance. He stood up quickly, and when a meaty fist rocketed toward his face, Tom dodged left. Tackling the monster, he head-butted him in the gut, then he bulldozed Tattoo upward, flipping him over. Tom stood victoriously, watching the brute struggle on the ground. He felt the adrenaline surging in his veins with every heaving breath.

To his amazement, Tattoo arose and, like an angry pit-bull, charged with all his might. His arm was cocked back, ready to wield a deadly blow. At the last second, Tom turned, and Tattoo bashed the outside of the cave with a jarring thud.

While Tattoo shook his hand in pain, Tom lunged for the knife, which was four feet to his left. Tattoo's steely fingers snagged his ankle and yanked him to the rock floor facedown. Rolling onto his back, Tom positioned his feet into a battering ram and aimed both boots at Tattoo's knee. He heard the sound of bones cracking and the big man grunting in agony.

Somehow, Tattoo managed to slam his enormous torso across Tom's chest in a tight straddle, his massive hands around his throat. Tom gasped for air in frustration. He hadn't seen that coming. Tom considered his opponent. He had to give the bastard points. Most dudes pass out when someone brakes their kneecap.

Somehow, Tattoo managed to slam his enormous torso down across Tom's chest. Tom gasped for air in frustration. He hadn't seen that coming.

Tattoo pinned Tom down in a tight straddle, his massive hands constricting his windpipe. Soon, black spots swirled in Tom's sight, and the world grayed at the edges. He tried to wedge his arms between the heavy, strangling iron bar forearms. Unable to loosen the steely grip, Tom gouged his thumbs into Tattoo's eyes. *It worked!* Tattoo let go with a furious growl. While he watched the ox lean backward in pain, Tom felt the air burn as he inhaled. He coughed as air filled his lungs and waited for Tattoo to recover and move forward, then with all his strength, Tom drove the heel of his hand into the guy's nose. Despite all the blood that gushed out, Tattoo reared backward in reflex. Tom bucked, flipping him face down. He heard another grunt. Tom took advantage of his opponent's weakness and dropped his knees on top of Tattoo. Tattoo collapsed in the dirt like a tent in a windstorm. Tom kneeled beside the defeated bulk and gasped for air, but

Tattoo wasn't out for the count. While Tom began to scan the area for Lisa, Scratch, and the park rangers, Tattoo rose up and smashed his fist into the side of Tom's head.

Stars exploded in Tom's vision. The hulk scissor-kicked his legs and twisted until he and Tom were locked in a deadly embrace. They rolled across the cold, hard rock, grappling for a superior position.

Tom threw punches left and right. A few grazed the intended target, bruising his knuckles. Punches flew toward him.

Tom's head snapped back, absorbing a wicked blow to the jaw.

Ow! That'll leave a mark.

Enraged, Tom thought, *time to close down the ballpark.*

He thrust away, reared up behind his enemy, and flung an arm around the thick neck, wedging it in the crook of his elbow. Using his body as a lever against Tattoo's weight, he pulled back and squeezed, compressing both carotid arteries. Tattoo thrashed, sending the battle into extra innings.

Bruising elbows pummeled Tom's ribs, but he hung on. The sleeper hold did its job. The fight drained out of his captive. Finally, Tattoo went limp.

Tom dropped the unconscious brute to the rock floor.

Three strikes and you're out, pal.

Suddenly, Tom thought about the knife. Dragging his aching, sweat-soaked body along the ground, he hoped Scratch wouldn't grab it first. Tom had never felt so lucky as he placed his hands around the handle of the knife. He pushed to his feet to wield the knife toward Scratch. He wasn't there. Neither was Lisa.

Where'd they go? Did he take her and run off?

Suddenly, a cold, dead feeling ran down his spine. He had to find her. Fast.

CHAPTER 26

Lisa watched Tattoo and Tom fight hand to hand combat. She was frightened. She hoped Tom would win. She couldn't help but gasp as Tom was hit in the jaw. *Oh! That should hurt!*

She was worried about him. She was about to yell to Tom when, suddenly, masculine hands were kneading her shoulders.

"They're too busy to bother with us," Scratch said with a sultry, sexy voice. "Let's go over there and talk awhile."

She knew immediately that talking was *not* what he had in mind. She shivered, scared. What was she going to do?

She turned to look at him. How had she not seen the evil in him earlier? She had dismissed him by being more frightened of Tattoo. Icy, emotionless eyes made him seem even scarier. She tried to push past him. To get away.

"Don't leave just yet," he purred. "Party's just getting started." His harsh mouth twisted, cruel intent gleaming in those bone-chilling eyes. He was going to kill her. She knew it, but first, he was going to rape her. This was not like Grey. He let her live, but he raped her. She froze back then, but this time, she was going to fight.

Dammit, she thought, *I'm going to fight even to the death.*

When Scratch pulled her close to kiss her with his wet, slobbery lips, she shivered. He paused to say, "I like it when you shiver." He smirked evilly. "It means you can't resist me." As Scratch leaned to kiss her, she turned her head. He growled, grabbing her hair. He ground up against her. The searing pain in her scalp made her eyes water. He pressed his dirty lips on her mouth. Lisa couldn't move.

She remembered the self-defense classes she had taken, but that was so long ago. *Why didn't I keep up with them?* she wondered. But at the time, she thought she had learned everything and would never need it again. *I've got to try it anyway.*

Lifting her leg, she kneaded him in the groin. He doubled over.

I did it!

"Bitch!" he hissed.

She reached down and grabbed a smoldering stick from the fire as she had seen Tom do and hoped she didn't burn her hand. Lisa hit Scratch on the head as he bent over, knocking him to the ground.

She sprinted past him, wondering where to hide. There was rock all around, nowhere to go. Suddenly, she noticed the brush in the distance. Lisa ran toward the maze of bushes and ferns. When she looked over her shoulder, however, Scratch was right behind her, cursing a litany of expletives. His rough hands snatched at her clothing. She could hear him breathing hard. Fear and momentum empowered her. She ran faster and sprinted into the brush.Surrounded by the heavy brush, Lisa slowed down. Darkness, terror, and the fight-or-flight reflex ricocheting through her veins disoriented her, but she pushed through. She had to.

"I like party games, girlie." Scratch's words vibrated with sick excitement.

Great. A whack job.

You didn't have to be psychotic to rape, but it probably helped during the killing part. Cold sweat dampened Lisa's skin as she weighed her options.

Hide?

Run?

Attack?

None seemed viable.

Scratch cajoled in an eerie sing-song voice, "Come out, come out, wherever you are…"

Defiantly closer.

Lisa held her breath. One small noise could get her killed.

"Now I'm bored," Scratch complained. It sounded like he was about fifteen feet behind her, but he'd veered off to the right.

Stay away, she prayed, shivering with fright.

"I hate being bored," he sneered.

She flinched, hearing the anger in his voice. Whacko Scratch was now a really ticked-off whacko Scratch. She darted in the opposite direction.

All at once, Lisa tripped over something and fell spread-eagle. Lisa risked looking back. It was a long piece of metal bar. She picked it up. It was heavy but not too heavy to carry—in case she needed it. Lisa pushed through the tall, heavy green stalks, determined to keep going. She had to keep away from the creep who'd stood twice in the brawn line and skipped the brains. Her duty at the moment was to survive.

Yet Lisa's lead-weight legs were flagged. She had hiked a long way the day before and now the strain of running away on an empty stomach had taken a toll. She forced herself to keep running. Lisa hesitated. She didn't want to get too far away from Tom though.

What if he wasn't okay? What if he needed her help? Maybe she should go back?

Soon, running footsteps pounded behind her, and she shot another look over her shoulder. Scratch, with his glacier eyes, was closing the distance. Fast and seething.

Her heart thundered. Dread streaked through her, and she poured on the speed. If he caught her, she'd be out of chances. She veered to the left to circle back to Tom. *Keep going.* The mistake sent shockwaves down Lisa's spine. Scratch had anticipated her moves and grabbed the back of her T-shirt, jerking her to a stop. *No! Oh, no! So close! I was sure I escaped him!*

He spun her around to face his fury. "Think you're clever?" he growled. Iron fingers clamped her shoulders, and he shook her until her spine nearly snapped. "I'm gonna teach you a lesson you'll never forget." His hand cracked across her face, the stinging blow knocking her to the dirt floor.

Dazed and gasping, Lisa sprawled in the sticky brush. She licked her lip and tasted blood. Her head spun, her face throbbed, and black spots swam in her vision. Down and fading fast. Helpless as a baby, she watched his expression contorted with hatred.

Scratch lunged at her and Lisa considered her life expectancy was about four or five minutes, which would probably seem like an eternity.

Just as she began to close her eyes, a savage war cry rang in her ears… and Tom hurtled out of the green brush. Narrowed blue eyes quickly scanned her, and the blistering rage in them sent her reeling.

"I'll kill you!" Tom charged and tackled Scratch. Elation winged through her.

Tom's okay! And looking plenty healthy.

His powerhouse jaw punch snapped the wacko's head back. Scratch grunted, staggered, then he rebounded and slugged Tom. She tried to scramble to her feet, but the stunning blow to her face had trashed her coordination. Scratch's fist rammed into Tom's stomach. How could he fight a second creep after Tattoo? Tom bent double, and Scratch whipped his gun from his ankle.

"Tom, gun!" she yelled. Tom's hands shot out, clamped the robber's wrist. The pistol waved wildly between them as they struggled for possession. The rapist aimed a vicious kick at Tom's knee. Tom dodged, deflecting the blow and knocking the gun out of Scratch's hand and into the sticky green brush.

All three of them dived for it. Lisa reached it first. She pulled it up by the handle and aimed it at Scratch. She grew up in Texas and had practiced shooting on her grandfather's farm, but that was years ago. She glanced at Tom. He reached out his hand, and she handed it to him.

"Up." Tom motioned with the gun for Scratch to raise his hands, which he did. "Move."

Scratch turned his back and started walking back to the rock. Tom reached his hand out and helped Lisa up and held her hand.

"He tried to rape me," she whispered, leaning toward Tom and knowing he'd be sympatric because of Grey's actions. "I was afraid he'd try to kill me too."

She felt Tom's hand clench… tight. *Ouch!* "Sorry," he said, keeping his eyes on Scratch. "I didn't mean to hurt you."

"It's okay," she said.

But it was not okay. As they walked back to the camp, Lisa wondered if she made a mistake in telling him what Scratch did.

Tattoo was still out cold when they arrived back at the campsite. Scratch turned around and looked at Tom.

"You do that?" he asked Tom, incredulous.

"Yeah," Tom stated angrily. "Want the same?"

"No, no. Just asking," Scratch responded.

"Sit down!" Tom said. "Cross your legs and put your hands behind your back.

Suddenly, two uniformed park rangers drove up in four-wheelers. One was riding a Yamaha Wolverine 350 ATV and the other, a Honda TRX420FM1 4Trax Ranger. Quickly removing their helmets, the rangers pulled out rifles and pointed them at Tom, who was holding a gun on Scratch.

"What's going on?" one of the park rangers shouted.

"These two tried to hold us up and rape my girlfriend," Tom answered. "I just beat up that one and wrestled this gun away from this one," he said, waving the gun at Scratch.

"Give us the gun," one ranger said.

"Yes, sir," Tom answered, handing over the gun to the second ranger who stepped up to take it.

"What's your story?" he asked Scratch.

"We were just having some fun, officer," Scratch spoke up, still sitting on the ground with his hands behind his back. He smirked like he would get away with this.

"Yeah," Tattoo added, waking up and pushing his way into a sitting position. "We didn't mean any harm. These two just took it the wrong way."

When he heaved himself off the rock and started to walk toward the rangers, Lisa and Tom both yelled, "No!"

"That's close enough," the second ranger said, speaking to Tattoo, over Lisa and Tom's protests. "Were these guys bothering you?" He looked at Tom and Lisa.

"Yes," Lisa said.

"No," Tom said at the same time, then they looked at each other.

"Well, which is it?" Ranger Adams asked.

"Yes," Tom said sheepishly as he hung his head. "They were bothering us."

"Yes," Lisa spoke up angrily. "They both have knives and were boxing us in. That one," pointing at Scratch, "tried to rape me." He hit me upside the head."

"Is that where the handprint came from?" the ranger asked.

"There's a handprint on my face?" Lisa asked, turning to Tom.

"Sure is," Tom growled at Scratch. Tom reached up and touched Lisa's face tenderly, but she winced away in pain when he touched her.

"You two were…" Ranger Adams spoke up, looking at Tattoo and Scratch, "just having a little bit of fun, huh? You two look familiar. Don't they, Ranger Jones?"

"Yes, sir, they do, Ranger Adams."

"We weren't going to hurt 'em. Just scare 'em a little bit," Scratch drawled.

"Lay on the ground with your hands behind your backs. Now!" Ranger Jones snapped.

When Ranger Adams cocked his rifle, Tattoo and Scratch stiffened their bodies like a stone. Ranger Jones snapped handcuffs on Tattoo, then he put on some rubber gloves and searched his pockets and legs. In a few seconds, the ranger pulled out three knives, two pistols, three bags of white crystals in baggies, and his wallet.

Tom's eyes widened. *Why didn't the guy pull any of those out on him? He probably thought he could take me without them. We were lucky.*

"We'll just keep these," Ranger Adams said as they each put the weapons into the side pockets of their four-wheelers.

"You can't keep my wallet," Tattoo growled, still coughing.

"Why not? What's in here? Lots of money. Is it stolen?" Ranger Adams asked. "What about these baggies of white crystals? Coke?"

"No," Tattoo stated. "Of course not."

"We'll see about that. We'll have the lab test it out," Ranger Adams said.

"Are you two the hikers that got lost?" Ranger Adams asked, turning his attention to Tom and Lisa.

"Yes," Tom answered. "We were waiting for you and these two drove up. We don't have anything until I took that gun away from Scratch." Tom pointed to Scratch. "At least that's how he introduced himself. The other one never gave us a name, so we called him Tattoo because of the tattoo on his neck."

"Tattoo?" Tattoo roared. "I'm Snake!"

"We'll see about you," Ranger Adams said. "Be quiet for now."

Turning back to Tom and Lisa, Ranger Adams said, "Get on the back of our bikes and we'll leave." Lisa and Tom scrambled and headed that direction. Tom held tight onto Lisa's hand. Each got on the back of a four-wheeler.

"What about us?" Scratch wailed.

"Let's see. Who do we have here?" Ranger Adams looked at the wallets. "Henley and Beau."

Lisa giggled. "And I thought we had Tattoo and Scratch."

"Yeah, you have a tattoo on your neck, Snake, and you didn't introduce yourself," Tom answered.

"Think we ought to just leave them here, locked up like that?" Ranger Jones looked at Ranger Adams, turning back and winking at Lisa and Tom. Tom looked at Lisa. They each had gotten on the four-wheelers, but he now moved over to her side.

"How are you doing?" he asked a still-pale-and-shaken Lisa, reaching for her hand. She let him put his arm around her and pull her close. "I'm so sorry I didn't get there before he hit you, sweetheart." He looked at her and gently pulled her face to look at him.

"You got there as fast as you could," Lisa said, ducking her head.

"Look at me, sweetheart," Tom said, touching the cheek that was not hurt. "I want to see those beautiful blue eyes looking at mine," he coached softly. An unsteady hand reached up, and he caressed her tender bottom lip with his thumb. "Fuckwad drew blood on my woman. That's a killing offense."

"Easy there, cowboy. Don't go all *Braveheart* on me."

"He hit you. Put his hands on you." Furious eyes glittered hotly. "I wanted to make him hurt, baby. Bad."

"I know." Surprisingly, she'd felt equally furious when she saw Tattoo hurting him. Even more surprising, she accepted full-blown rage. No shame. No guilt. She gently kissed his warm, bristly cheek. He wasn't the only one who possessed the instinct to protect his mate.

"Wow!" She almost smiled. "You really knocked the crap out of Tattoo! And Snake! Where did you learn to fight like that? You saved us both!"

"I… uh… I learned at the gym I go to. But I only practice there," Tom hedged. "I've never fought for real. For my life," he paused. "Or for someone else, like you, baby."

"I was so terrified you were going to get hurt." She reached up and touched his jaw.

Tom flinched. "Ouch." He grinned. "Guess I did get hurt."

"Now we've got matching faces," Lisa giggled as tears slipped out of her eyes.

"Don't cry, beautiful. They're caught, and we're moving on." Tom leaned Lisa's head down on his shoulder. "Better still, just let it all out," Tom soothed, pulling her closer.

Now, Lisa felt as if everything was going to be okay and turned her attention back to the rangers.

"Sure. We can just leave them here. Let the wild hogs get them," Ranger Adams answered Ranger Jones.

"You can't just leave us locked up out here," Tattoo growled.

"Why not? You were aggravating these people. Maybe we should just take them in?" Ranger Jones asked, looking at Ranger Adams.

"Yeah…" Ranger Adams sighed and rubbed his hand over his mouth. "But we have to get someone out here to carry them in." He picked up his radio and called. "Base Station, come in. Base Station, come in. Over."

"Base Station here, over," the radio squawked.

"We have two felons that were picking on our hikers, with knives and pistols…"

"We didn't pull out our pistols on them!" Scratch called out.

"Shut up, Scratch!" Tattoo yelled.

"Yes, you did," Lisa spoke up.

"One is named Henley Foster and the other is Beau Jacob. Do they have any outstanding warrants?"

"One moment, please. Do they have license numbers?"

"Yes." Ranger Adams rattled off the license numbers on the drivers' licenses.

"Yup, they sure do. Both for B&E, speeding, resisting arrest, and aggravated assault. Bring them in."

"We will need a wagon to pick them up. We have the felons handcuffed and lying on the ground right now, but we have the two lost hikers with us. We can stay out here and watch them until the wagon shows up," Ranger Adams said.

"No, tie them to a tree and we'll send the wagon on around. It'll take too long for you to wait for the wagon to get there. We're sending it out now. That way, you can go ahead and bring the hikers on in and start on their statements," the radio squawked more.

"We don't have trees out here," Ranger Adams chuckled. "This area is close to Makauwahi Cave and a rocky area. There's a cave, but no trees. There are also bushes within sight, but no trees."

"If you don't tie up their feet, they'll run away," the radio squawked.

"We'll figure something out. Over and out."

"Roger. Over and out," the radio squawked off.

"Well, boys, it looks like you're going to be tied up." Ranger Adams smiled as he pulled his rope out of his pouch.

"You can't do that to us," Scratch groaned.

"Stay there, boys. We'll tie you up real good," Ranger Jones snarled as he continued to hold his rifle on them.

Ranger Adams walked over to Snake and handcuffed his feet together, then he tied both his hands and feet with a rope over the handcuffs, then he tied a rope between the hands and the feet, effectively hog-tying him, his hands behind him. He did the same to Scratch, leaving both on their stomachs. Tom moved back to the other bike. The rangers put away their rifles and got on their bikes in front of Tom and Lisa.

"What are your names?"

"I'm Tom Jefferys, and this is Lisa Collins."

"We're Ranger Jones and Adams. Ready to go, guys?" Ranger Adams said.

"Yes," Tom said. "Let's get out of here."

CHAPTER 27

They pulled into the ranger station on the four-wheelers. Olive, Mason, Emma, Noah, and Sophia came running out to greet them.

"Oh, Lisa!" Olive exclaimed as Lisa climbed off of the bike. "I'm so glad you're safe!"

Emma and Sophia grabbed and hugged her. "We were so worried!"

Mason, Noah, and Bill shook Tom's hand. "You went exploring, huh?" Bill teased. "I guess you won't be doing that again."

"Probably not," Tom said, embarrassed. He felt responsible for what happened. Lisa could have been raped or, worse, killed.

She's alive and safe, he reminded himself, staring at Lisa who was surrounded by the girls. He could never forgive himself if she had been harmed. When Lisa turned to face him, Tom grinned, unable to contain his relief.

"Tom beat up both bandits," Lisa announced proudly to the group. "He did hand-to-hand combat with one guy and wrestled a gun away from the other."

"Well, we wrestled until the gun hit the ground, but Lisa grabbed it," Tom corrected, smiling. "She's quite the Annie Oakley."

"Had quite an adventure, didn't you!" Emma exclaimed. "How romantic!"

"There was no romance in getting hit and almost killed!" Lisa replied, pointing at her face.

"Lisa!" Sophia gasped, leaning over to get a closer look. "Is that a handprint?"

Suddenly, Lisa's voice cracked. "It's from the guy who had the gun. He was… holding me down," she stammered. "And he was… trying… to…" Lisa broke down, unable to complete her sentence.

"Oh, sweetie," Olive cried. She grabbed Lisa, who buried her face in Olive's shoulder. The girls knew that Lisa had been raped in the past and quickly gathered around her in an unspoken band of support, as if they wanted to banish the horrific experience from her mind.

Bill, Noah, and Mason all stood as they watched, their mouths open and bewildered and then they looked at Tom.

Mason scanned Tom from top to bottom. "You beat up two guys?" he asked with an expression of wonderment that might have been insulting under different circumstances, like responding to a tall tale told at a bar.

Listening to Lisa cry, however, Tom hung his head. "Yeah."

"You're a hero!" Bill said, punching Tom playfully on the arm. "At least to her," he chuckled, eliciting laughter from the guys.

Tom tried not to wince at Bill's firm slap. Until then, he hadn't felt the pain of his injuries.

"You saved both of your lives out there," Mason said.

When Mason reached over to pat him on the back, however, Tom instinctively moved away. "Sorry, Mason. It was a fight to the death."

"Wow," Noah said.

"So you don't need to go to the hospital or something? I mean, wow, Tom. Are you gonna' be all right?" Bill asked.

"Oh yeah, yeah," Tom said, putting on a brave face. "I just need to get some rest."

While the guys nodded slowly in unison, Tom kept his ears peeled to Lisa. He only wanted her to be all right.

"But I fought back," Lisa said, sniffling as she pulled away from Olive's shoulder.

"You did?" Olive said.

"Yes. And you know what?" Lisa said, her eyes widening with a watery smile. "I think I feel stronger now about what happened before. Isn't that weird? I actually have a different… I don't know, I just feel stronger now.

"Oh, honey." Olive smiled. "You've always been strong."

"Lisa," Emma said. You're a survivor".

The girls nodded, but now, Lisa didn't pretend as she agreed. She did believe them.

"I know I can only guess how much you suffered, but despite that creep, you've come back, stronger and more confident. Look at all the things you've accomplished since then. He could never defeat you," Sophia added.

"You're right," Lisa said, smiling at her friends. "Thanks."

While the girls separated from their huddle, Olive announced, "Now that you two are back we need to go catch our plane back to Maui so we can finish this trip." When Olive noticed the big eyes and gaping mouths, she realized how flippant it must have sounded. "I didn't mean that I haven't enjoyed this fantastic trip. We just need to go. I'm looking forward to our bike tour tomorrow! Aren't you?"

Everyone relaxed.

"Yes, it'll be fun!" exclaimed Emma.

Tom immediately sought Lisa and swallowed his pain to give her a side hug.

A bike tour, he thought, wondering if he could assess his injuries on the plane.

***

The group rode in the van back to the hotel and packed up. They left soon afterward to go to the airport to catch their flight back to Maui. On the flight, Tom raised the armrest between them, and Lisa snuggled into him. This was a little island hopper and did not have first-class seats. It was only a two-hour flight. The buddy moon group landed and caught a van to the hotel. The same hotel they'd been in before. Luckily, they managed to get the same rooms next to each other. Two three-room suites, with an en-suite bath each, living room, and kitchenette.

"We'll meet you downstairs in the pool," Lisa suggested when they stood at the girl's suite door. "I haven't practiced my swimming enough on this vacation."

"Sounds good to me." Tom nodded slowly. "Then I can see you in your bathing suit again."

"What about all that snorkeling and swimming we did in Kauai and last week here in Maui?" Tom heard Sophia say.

"Oh, you know I'm a fish and need water! I have to be swimming all the time," Lisa replied, who winked at Tom as she closed the door.

He smiled, thinking about how much he loved his little fish. *Loved? Is that how I feel?* Those words didn't make him want to run for the hills nor get far away from her. Not like Maria, who wore heavy perfume. He always felt closed in by Maria, but he felt open and free with Lisa, who smelled like lilacs. *Maybe love did cover it.* His smile got bigger as he entered his room to dress for the pool.

Tom, Bill, and Noah got to the pool before everyone else.

"Let's do cannonballs!" Noah yelled and ran for the pool, splashing as he jumped in.

"Is he five?" Bill asked, turning to Tom.

"Yes-s-s," Tom said.

Bill chuckled.

"What's taking the girls so long?" Tom asked.

"You mean, what's taking Lisa so long, right?" Bill said.

Tom snapped his towel, jokingly at Bill. Just then, Maria strutted in front of Tom and stopped. "Tommy!" she cried, her voice changing to husky. "I thought you were in Kawai."

He took one look at her and felt sick, not turned-on like he might have been before he met Lisa. Maria looked desperate for the kind of attention she usually wanted and got from all the guys she slept with, including his ex-friend. He watched her turn sideways to show off her body like she usually did around men. She was wearing a red bathing suit as her breasts hung out precariously and her butt cheeks stuck out perfectly round and naked. Tom suspected it was one of those thong things women wore when they wanted to look sexy, yet he didn't care if Maria was completely nude; she couldn't compare to Lisa.

"We were, Maria," he answered cordially. "But now we're back, for the rest of today, tomorrow, and Saturday when we fly home.".

"Oh, so do I," Maria answered in her sultry voice, leaning over to push her breasts into his arm. I'm here for the next three days too. Maybe we'll be on the same plane. Maybe we can sit together."

"I think we have assigned seats on the flight home," Tom said, feeling like a fly caught in a sticky strip.

"Well, maybe our seats are together," Maria purred. "Let's hope."

Tom flinched. *I hope not*, he thought as he felt his body respond to her sexy body. It made no sense. He knew he didn't want her, but Maria hung all over him and he wasn't sure how to dislodge her.

I just fought two men and yet I can't push this woman off me.

Suddenly, Lisa appeared, stopping him in mid-thought.

"Lisa," he called out.

"Tom." She gave a stiff nod, a tinge of hurt in her fiery glare. "Hello, Maria."

"We were just—" He looked at her helplessly.

"Please. Don't let me interrupt."

Tom heard the icy tone dripping off Lisa's tongue as she strode off. He also noticed the girls had lined up behind her.

First, Sophia followed suit. "Right!" She frowned, flipping her hair at Tom as she turned to leave. "Have fun."

One-by-one, the girls expressed their disgust at Tom.

Mason and Olive began to walk away too. When Mason paused, however, Olive let go of his arm to join Lisa and the girls at the pool.

Mason shook his head at Tom. "Trying to get yourself in trouble?" he asked, tilting his head oddly at Maria's forehead, as if he wanted to avoid any sight of the boobs that looked like they were being served on a platter. He nodded and moved on.

"Get off me, Maria," Tom said, pushing her arm away so she would no longer drape herself all over him.

"Awe, Tommy," Maria said. "She's just jealous of me. Because I have you."

"You do not *have* me, Maria," Tom said. "I love Lisa. You and I are just friends. That's all we'll ever be."

"That's not the impression I got when we were in Olive's room together back in the dorm. How could you love Lisa?" she spat. "How dare you blow me off like trash! All this time, I've been waiting for you. That's years, Tom. Years! And now? Now you want to drop me for some skinny witch you just met. Huh?" she asked, her voice almost a scream. "Is that what you're doing, Tom?"

"We were never together like that, and you know it! What about that guy? What's his name? We were both dating other people, so I don't see how you can think we had some big love affair. I like you, Maria. Always have. But… there is no us. Never was. Come on, Maria. You know it's true. Can we at least be friends?

"Hmph! Keep your skinny witch!" Maria huffed. "And *friends!* I don't want you as a friend!" Maria stomped away and went toward the pool. "I'm going swimming."

Tom looked at Bill.

"Well, that went well," Bill deadpanned.

"Yeah, right," Tom answered. "Now I have two women mad at me."

"That's what happens when you play the field, fella," Bill said.

"But I'm not playing the field… anymore," Tom huffed.

"Maria was… you know."Bill nodded, gazing at Maria.

"Since I've been with Lisa these past two weeks, I don't want to date anyone else."

"Been with?" Bill grinned, raising an eyebrow.

Tom's adrenaline rose up in his throat. "Lisa is not like that!" He frowned. "She not a— She's nothing like Maria."

"Okay, calm down. I get it. But you said you *love* her." Bill smirked. "Have you told her yet?"

"No, I just figured it out," Tom said. "You and Maria are the first to know. Not Lisa." Tom bit the inside of his mouth.

"Hope Maria doesn't get to Lisa before you do, bud," Bill said. "She's fuming. She's liable to say anything. And it could be bad."

Tom hadn't considered that. He better get to Lisa, even if she wasn't talking to him… *especially* if she wasn't talking to him.

CHAPTER 28

Lisa saw Maria hanging all over Tom, and the green-eyed monster grabbed her. She knew she felt jealous and was fuming. He kept saying they were just friends, but Maria was always there. Maria had been here all vacation. Well, not all vacation, just the wedding and now. She had not been in Hana, Maui, or Kawai. *Thank God.* But she was here, and Lisa was irritated. She had overheard Maria say that she hoped to be on the same flight with Tom, sitting beside him. *Ooooh.*

"Are you all right, Lisa?" Sophia asked after the girls sat down by the swimming pool. They dangled their feet in the water.

Lisa huffed. "No."

"You do know he's got a reputation, don't you?" Emma asked.

"What kind of reputation?" Lisa asked, concerned.

"You know, dating lots of girls. Sometimes for a whole week," Sophia said. "Then breaking up with them."

Lisa turned to her friend. "Did you know that, Olive?"

"Well, yes, I did. But Mason said he had changed last year and was looking to be more settled down. Dating only one girl for a while. No more one-night stands."

"One-night stands?" Lisa's eyes went wide. She was horrified. She could have been his one-night stand, but she'd pushed him away. He kept kissing her and pushing her. He said he wouldn't push her, but he did. More than kissing, he got her to let him touch her breast. She was perplexed. He had talked her into telling him what she wanted. But did she really? Was she being manipulated? She wasn't sure she wanted to be with Tom anymore. He had saved her from getting raped, but he's the one who got them lost… just so he could neck with her. She was very confused. And angry.

Maria walked up. "Lisa," she said. "Did you hear? Tom and I are together now."

Lisa gasped.

"Yes, we're going to sit together on the plane ride home," Maria continued. "Won't you be on the same plane?"

"Maria," Olive said to her cousin, "I think it's time for you to go."

"But I just wanted to let Lisa know that Tom and I used to be just friends, but now we're boyfriend and girlfriend. He *loves* me. He said so," Maria said, ignoring Olive.

Lisa squinted her eyes at Maria angrily.

"Move along now, Maria," Sophia said. "We all know that's not true. You've been saying that for years. Ever since you met him when you were seventeen. He doesn't love you any more than just as a friend."

"Oh, yes." Maria smirked wickedly. "He just asked me to be his girlfriend. Ask him. He can't deny it. He'll trip all over his words trying to continue to get into your pants, Lisa, but he's mine. Not yours. Forget him."

"Why would you want him if you think he is chasing someone else *after* he asked you to be his girlfriend? Huh, Maria? Sounds fishy to me. Maybe you are lying just to get to Lisa," Emma asked.

"He wants me and me alone," Maria huffed. "And don't you forget it." With that, Maria got up and left, making sure to sashay her butt-cheeks seductively as she walked away.

"What am I going to do?" Lisa wailed quietly.

"Ask Tom," Olive suggested. "I tell you, Mason said he changed. He is tired of one-night stands, women who are not interested in long-term relationships, or gold-diggers. He is looking to settle down. Ask him. Listen to his answers."

"Maybe," Lisa huffed, still not convinced.

"Lisa," Tom said. "Can we talk?"

She realized he had walked over.

"About what?" Lisa asked, still angry at him and envious of Maria. She wanted Tom, but not if he was a Casanova. She didn't want to be one of many. She wanted to be the only one. She had thought—for two weeks—she was. How stupid of her.

"Lisa," Tom coaxed. "I think we really need to talk. Privately. Please."

When she noticed Olive nodding encouragingly, Lisa stood up. "Oh, all right," she grudgingly agreed.

Tom tried to take her hand, but she put it behind her and refused to touch him. They walked over to the ocean and sat away from the pool, away from her friends. But still out in the open. *Good.* He wouldn't begin kissing her and making her want him. Lisa breathed deeply to control her anger and disappointment.

There were patio tables and bench seating. There were lawn chairs on the beach too. Lisa headed for the lawn chairs. Tom followed her. Lisa sat down and relaxed. Falsely. Tom sat sideways on the lawn chair, his legs apart and his hands clenched together in fists between his knees with his head hanging down.

"Lisa, sweetheart," he began, lifting his head and looking at her.

"Don't sweetheart me," Lisa spat at him, turning in his direction. "I just heard about you. You date girls for a week and then move on. What was I? Your Hawaiian vacation girlfriend?"

"No!" Tom answered, sounding confused and angry. "You're so much more than that to me. I've enjoyed—"

"Enjoyed what? Kissing me? Trying to sleep with me?"

"No! Our time together has been so special—"

But Lisa wouldn't have it. Maria embarrassed her and his reputation too.

"I don't want to be your two-week date of convenience in Hawaii and then never see you again," Lisa said.

"That's not the way it is, Lisa!" Tom started. "Why won't you listen to me?"

"I don't know what to say to you, Tom," Lisa mumbled. "Maria said you asked her to be your girlfriend," Lisa said quietly, thinking, *you didn't ask me that.*

"No!" Tom almost shouted. "I didn't ask Maria to be my girlfriend. I asked her to consider me as her friend. She doesn't listen."

"That's what she was telling me when you walked up," Lisa said.

"Wow," he whispered. "That's not true. I had just been talking to her, telling her we could always be friends but not anything more."

"Have you ever been with her?"

"No!" Tom said, wrinkling his nose in disgust. He paused and dropped his head. He reached out for Lisa's hand. She moved so he couldn't touch her.

"I met Maria in college," Tom started. "She was a senior in high school, age seventeen. I was a senior in college. Olive had her up for a football party weekend. She was also there to see the college she wanted to attend the following year."

Lisa looked up at Tom, trying to decide if she wanted to believe him.

"Maria must have gotten separated from Olive," Tom continued, "because she was pretty soused. She was wobbling around, stumbling, and slurring her words. I couldn't find Olive, and I didn't want to leave Maria alone. If I'd left her alone, I didn't know who might latch onto a teenager and take advantage of her. Rape her. And I didn't want to sit with her for hours, hoping Olive would just *happen* to show up. I didn't have Olive's phone number then, but I did know where her dorm room was. I took her there."

Lisa squinted her eyes. Was he really plausible?

"I was also afraid to be alone with her actually."

"Why was that?" Lisa asked.

"She was seventeen. Jail bait."

"Oh?"

"If I was found alone with her and someone realized she was seventeen, I knew I could be taken to jail for child molestation. Just because she was underage. And we were not just three years apart, but five years apart. I knew that the law said that if a child—boy or girl—dates or is alone with someone three years older, then the older *adult* would be taken in for child molestation. No excuses. You're guilty because you're caught."

"Wow."

"Anyway. As I said, she was stumbling and slurring her words. No control. I tried to put her to bed. She decided I was her knight in shining armor and kept trying to kiss me. I finally wrestled her into bed, then she removed her dress. Thank goodness she had on a full slip. So I found a pink, cat T-shirt in her drawer and put it over her head.

"Hello Kitty?" Lisa asked.

"What?"

"It's a pink cat T-shirt," Lisa said, smiling.

"Okay. Anyway," Tom finished. "I put that on her over her slip and didn't *see* anything inappropriate. I didn't *want* to see anything. And left. She seemed to think we did something sexy, and I was her boyfriend from then on. Now she claims she's twenty, of age, and is waiting for me to ask her out."

"I'm sorry that you had to put up with that, Tom," Lisa sighed, frustrated with the whole story. "But why should I listen to a liar?" Lisa quarreled with him.

"How did I lie?" Tom challenged.

"You didn't tell me you really are a man who does one-night stands. Or one-week dates. Then you move on."

Tom hung his head. "You're right. I didn't tell you about my past. I was afraid that you'd find out and not like me anymore," he said, in defeat.

"See, that's a lie," Lisa stated.

"How? I didn't mention it," he said. "You didn't ask me about it. I didn't deny it!"

"It was a lie of omission," Lisa challenged. "You could have brought it up. We talked about our pasts. You talked about your bullying and how you overcame it, but you never mentioned anything about being a Casanova."

"Lisa…" Tom began.

"You want to talk?" Lisa confronted. "Talk!"

"Lisa, sweet…"

Lisa shot him a hateful look.

Tom cleared his throat. "Lisa, yes, I have dated a lot of women."

"See? What I heard was right."

"Are you going to let me finish?

"Yes," she said, glaring at him.

"I've had lots of dates and lots of one-night stands. I didn't believe in love. I didn't think any woman would meet my expectations. Or touch my heart. I played around."

"Have you ever had a girlfriend?" Lisa asked, not quite so angry but not quite believing him either.

"In high school, I had a girlfriend, but I cheated on her," Tom confessed. "She broke up with me when she found out. I was a jerk then and didn't think it was my fault. That was after I grew a foot taller and developed muscles and the girls noticed me. They came on to me, and I fell for everyone. Every line. Every lie. I should have told you."

"You certainly should have," Lisa said. "That's a big deal, Tom."

Tom hung his head. "Yes, you're right, bab… uh, Lisa," Tom stuttered as he looked up at her again.

When Lisa heard Tom choke on his usual endearment, she couldn't help notice the care he was taking to choose the right words. She covered her mouth to not let him see her smile. She didn't want him to think he was forgiven. Yet.

"I learned in college that I shouldn't date. I shouldn't have a girlfriend because I would cheat. I started having one-night stands and figured I couldn't cheat if I only had sex with random girls. Cheating made me feel awful. Dirty. One-night stands didn't," Tom continued.

Lisa just looked at him, feeling distrust. She just didn't want to believe him. "Sounds like a convenient excuse," she said, her voice dripping with sarcasm.

"Okay, Lisa, it was the coward's way out, but it got me through," Tom admitted.

She scowled. "Lisa," he sighed. "You changed me. I don't want to have any more one-night stands or one-week dates any longer. I've been tired of that lifestyle for the past year and have been thinking of trying to change, but none of the girls I was with or met interested me. You are the only girl in the last six months that I have dated. Ask Mason!" he cried.

"I'm sorry that you've been through so much, Tom," Lisa sighed, frustrated with the whole situation. "Now that I escaped Snake and fought him off and you saved me, I feel stronger. I feel like I can do anything. Like I can date again. I wanted it to be you, but with Maria hanging around all the time and your answers…" she paused. "I actually do believe you about Maria. But still. The whole deal about your lie by omission bothers me. What else will you not tell me?"

"Nothing!" Tom exclaimed.

"And I just don't see how that relates to me," Lisa said. "Maybe I should just go."

CHAPTER 29

"No, Lisa! Wait!" Tom reached out his hand and placed it on her arm to stop her.

"For what?" Lisa snapped at him, pulling her arm away.

Tom scratched the back of his neck. He was so worried. "The thing is, Lisa…" Tom sighed. "I spilled something to Maria that made her jealous of you."

"Well, I've always suspected she was jealous of me," Lisa responded. "Not to seem egotistical, but I always thought that's why she attacked me and wouldn't let me apologize or agree to disagree."

"This was today," Tom said.

"Today?" Lisa snorted. "She's been after me for years."

"But today I realized something, and it's been coming on me for two weeks now," Tom said.

"What's that?" Lisa asked.

Tom ducked his head and sat up closer to her. He raised his head. Again, he reached for her hand. She stiffened, but she let him take it.

"Lisa, sweetheart…" Tom started.

She just looked at him.

He felt nervous. He ran his other hand through his hair. "Lisa, I love you."

"What?" Lisa asked.

"Yes, baby, I love you," Tom said shyly. "I realized it today. And I foolishly said it out loud in front of Maria, then she wrapped herself all over me just as you walked by."

"She did look back and see me approaching," Lisa said. "She smiled and wrapped herself all around you."

"See, it wasn't me."

"But you didn't push her away," Lisa said.

Tom sensed that Lisa was hurt, not angry or jealous. I see her as a friend, Lisa," Tom said. "I was trying to remind her, but she ignored me."

"She will always ignore you, Tom," Lisa said sadly. "She will always hang onto you. I can't put up with a cheat and a woman who constantly hangs all over him."

"But you love me too, don't you?"

Lisa looked up with tears in her eyes. "Yes, but I know better than to try to change you."

"But I can change," Tom moaned, swallowing his tears. "Please let me."

"No," Lisa whispered. "Tom, I love you, but I don't like your reputation. You have some growing up to do. You need to make sure I'm who you want, and not just the flavor of the week and not just a challenge because I don't give in right away. I did in the beginning, but I won't now. Check on me in five or six months. I'll always love you, but I want someone who will love me back… forever. Look me up when you change. Maybe then. Maybe. Till then…"

Lisa jumped up and ran past Tom into the ocean.

He stood there, stunned and dejected. After finally mustering the courage to tell her how he felt, she had rejected him. Well, not totally, but she was holding his past against him. Five or six months? That was an eternity! He wanted to move on with her now, with the love of his life.

He could see Lisa splashing in the water. He saw the big fat tears well up in her eyes. She loved him, but she was stepping back and waiting for him to be ready. Otherwise, she would end up terribly hurt.

"Is everything okay?" Sophia asked as she waded out to meet her.

Not ready to talk, Lisa gave a small nod.

Tom looked up and heard Bill talking.

"Let's check our hotel keycards in with the hotel desk clerk out here," Bill said.

"Is that why he's here?" Noah asked.

"Yes, you check your keycards and wallets and anything you don't want to leave on your towel on the beach or at the pool," Sophia said.

All, but Lisa and Tom, walked up and put their things in the basket and stepped back. The desk clerk handed the token to Sophia. "And you keep up with the token," she said, handing it to Bill.

"Why me?" Bill asked, taking a step backward.

"Because you look responsible," Noah answered him, laughing. "Take it."

Bill laughed and took the tokens. And they all wandered to the beach.

Noah, Bill, Olive, and Mason dropped their towels by Emma and Sophia's. They also brought Lisa a towel. They dropped the lotion they'd brought on the towels and ran to the waves. Tom decided to join them. No sign of Maria. *Thank God.*

They played in the water, jumping with each wave as it came in. Sophia returned to the shore and applied more sunscreen lotion. Bill came barreling out of the water and picked up Sophia and ran to the water.

"Put me down!" she declared, screaming and laughing at the same time, then he dropped her into the water. "You! I'll get you!" she sputtered, coming up. Sophia jumped up in the water and tried to dunk Bill, but all she accomplished was to put her hands on his head and raise herself in the air. He was standing on the bottom and didn't go under.

Tom looked at Lisa who also had come out of the water to get more sunscreen. "Oh, no you don't!" Lisa cautioned, still not in the mood to play.

Tom just smirked. "Are you telling me I can't do something?"

"I'm telling you that you better not!" Lisa warned, but her mouth was twitching at the corners.

"You are?" Tom asked, smiling, then he suddenly picked up Lisa and ran toward the water.

"Put me down!" Lisa screamed, but she held her breath as he tossed her in the water.

Then Noah did the same thing to Emma. They splashed and tried to dunk each other over and over again. The men tossed the women in the water several more times.

"Oh, a jellyfish just floated by," Lisa said, more to herself than to anyone else.

Then Tom grabbed Lisa and tossed her one more time into the water, away from that jellyfish.

She came up screaming, "It hurts! It hurts!" She started running toward the shore as fast as the water would let her go. "What hurts?" Tom shouted.

"My legs! My legs!" she screamed.

"What happened?" Tom asked, trying to soothe Lisa. She sat on her towel and tried to rub her legs, but as she'd reach out, she would pull her hand back as if it hurt too much to touch them, Tom observed. "What can I do?"

A stranger walked up. "There is a bloom of jellyfish out there," he said.

"There are?" Lisa cried softly through tears.

"There were? I am so sorry!" Tom said. "I didn't see them!"

Emma, Sophia, Bill, and Noah also came out of the water. "What happened?" Emma asked.

"Tom threw me into a bunch of jellyfish," Lisa sobbed.

"I'm sorry," Tom whispered, putting his arm around Lisa and pulling her close to his side.

"I know you didn't mean to," Lisa answered, looking up at him.

"I'll go see if the desk clerk knows what to do," Sophia said, running away. Tom spoke in a low voice that only Lisa could hear. "I really didn't see those jellyfish."

"I know," Lisa answered, trying not to cry. "I saw one but not a whole school of them."

"He said they were called a bloom, not school," Noah spoke up.

"Oh," Lisa said.

In a few minutes, Sophia came back with the hotel nurse. She had a bag and sat it down beside Lisa. "What is your name? she asked.

"Lisa."

"Okay, Lisa, tell me what happened," the nurse asked.

"The guys had been tossing us into the water, then I noticed a jellyfish. Then he tossed me again and I hurt. I noticed a lot of jellyfish floating by as I ran out of the water. I thought they were harmless. I came out, and my legs just hurt," she whimpered. Big tears spilled out of her eyes.

"It's just your legs? Not your arms or face? Nothing else hurts but your legs?" the nurse asked.

"That's right," Lisa answered.

"Okay. We have baking soda," the nurse said, pulling a large box of baking soda out of her bag. Turning to Tom, she handed him an empty water bottle and said, "Go fill this up with water from the ocean. And hurry."

Tom hurried over to the seashore and waded in until he could fill up the water bottle. He hurried back. "Here," he said, handing the water bottle to the nurse.

The nurse put on thin plastic gloves, then she poured the saltwater over Lisa's legs. Tom sat down beside Lisa and took her hand in his and squeezed. The nurse slathered baking soda all over her legs, from her thighs to her feet and in between her toes. "Okay, just sit here for a few minutes."

"This will help?" Noah asked as they all stood around watching.

"Yes," the nurse answered.

"Why saltwater?" Sophia asked.

"Freshwater seems to make the irritation worse. And saltwater seems to make it better. The tentacles of a jellyfish carry microscopic stingers. These stingers are injected with venom, which is the cause of the pain."

"Venom? Like a snake?" Emma asked.

"Yes, it's poison to our systems," the nurse answered. "Fortunately, humans are large enough that most reactions are redness and skin irritation. If it's worse, you should seek medical help. Yours looks like this will work. If a jellyfish floats by, don't bother it. It could result in what happened here. They were just defending themselves when you landed in the midst of them. The baking soda will loosen the stingers. When you rinse off in the ocean, the stingers will be removed. Are you ready?"

"Yes." Lisa breathed a big sigh.

"Okay, let's go get you rinsed off."

The nurse and Lisa started for the ocean. Tom grabbed Lisa's hand and held on. The nurse was wearing shoes, so she said, "Go rinse off in the water, Lisa. Do not brush it off with your hands. I'll do that later with gloves."

"Here, I'll go with you," Tom offered. They waded out into the ocean. The water rinsed off the baking soda. When Lisa came out, the nurse had changed gloves and asked Tom to fill up the water bottle again. There were a few spots that the baking soda did not just float away, so the nurse poured the water over it and brushed it away with her gloved hands.

"Come, sit down now and rest. Where the stingers were will be red and swollen for a few days. If it gets worse, come see me right away. Or better yet, call the front desk and have them call me. What's your room number?"

"We're in the Marianne Cottage," Sophia answered.

"I will tell the front desk to expect a call from you if you get worse. And for them to get in touch with me right away," the nurse said.

"We were planning on going home in two days," Bill spoke up to the nurse.

"That should be plenty of time to tell if the redness and swollen areas are okay and you're able to travel. In fact, why don't you come to my office tomorrow?"

"Okay," Lisa said.

"I'll go with you tomorrow, Lisa," Tom insisted.

"You don't have to," she answered. "I'm a big girl."

"Even big girls need help sometimes," he whispered.

She shivered, closed her eyes, and turned her head. "I'm going to my room," she said and started in that direction.

Tom fell into step with her.

Lisa remembered her disappointment and turned around. "You don't have to follow me everywhere I go. I really can take care of myself."

"I know," Tom said. "I just feel guilty for causing you pain."

Lisa looked ahead. "Don't worry about it," she said stoically.

"But I do worry about you, Lisa, and I love you. Please let me help."

"No," Lisa said, turning toward him. "No, Tom. I don't need your help. See me when you feel like you've changed, but don't take too long. I might have moved on by then."

With that, Lisa limped into the hotel.

CHAPTER 30

Lisa woke up early the next morning feeling fine. She jumped out of bed and looked down. There were red-looking lines running around her legs and up and down. They were not really welts but definitely red.

Great! How long is this going to last?

Emma gave a small knock and slid open the door to her bedroom. "Lisa, how are you doing this morning?"

Lisa showed off her legs.

"Oh, wow," Emma said, her mouth grimacing.

"I know." Lisa raised her eyebrows and smiled. "But the nurse said if it didn't hurt, I was good to go,"

Sophia walked in. "Whoa! Do you hurt?" she said, looking at Lisa's legs.

"Nope," Lisa said, popping the "*p*" at the end.

"What did you decide about the bike tour?" Sophia asked.

"I'm going!" Lisa exclaimed, a big smile on her face. "Let's call Olive and let her know."

The women got dressed and met Olive and Mason and the guys downstairs in time to be picked up for the early morning day bike tour.

"How are your legs?" Tom asked as soon as he saw Lisa. He walked up and hugged her. She stiffened a little but let him hug her. "Sophia told Bill you were doing better."

"They're fine." Lisa was a little fouler than she meant to be. She had promised to keep her distance from Tom until he changed his ways, but he was so close. She didn't want to be rude, and yet, she knew if he persisted, she'd forgive him. Maybe she should forgive him; it was the right thing to do, but she got the feeling he needed a challenge, something to work toward. And if he got too close, she'd give in. The van driver, of Hawaiian/Polynesian descent, stepped out of the van. "Aloha!" he called. "I'm Philipo, which is the Hawaiian form of Phillip, which means lover of horses. Come aboard, and I will tell you all about where we are going today and what you will be doing." He swept his arm toward the door of the van in a flourish.

The women got on the van first and Lisa went toward the back.

"Want to sit by me?" Sophia whispered.

"No," Lisa whispered back. "You want to sit by Bill."

Sophia smiled back, sort of sadly when Lisa shook her head.

The men got on the van next and all paired up. Tom came back to sit by Lisa. She looked up at him, challenging him to not sit by her, but he did anyway.

"Hi," he breathed.

"Hello," Lisa answered. "You know there is another seat you can take," she confronted him.

"Well, looka here, there sure is."

"Tom…"

"I want to sit by you," he interrupted. "It's a free country," she huffed, turning to stare out the window, away from Tom.

"Let me tell you about today's adventure," Philipo said. "You are going on a long bike tour that will take in the gorgeous vistas of Maui all around you."

Tom snuck his hand over Lisa's, tightening it before she could ply it out.

"We will start your escapade," Philipo continued, "at the 10,000-foot summit of Haleakala National Park and enjoy panoramic views of the crater. Since we are so early, you will see the sunrise at this elevation. At 6,500 feet, you will begin the actual bike ride, just outside the park boundary."

She turned to face Tom. He seemed so forlorn so she left her hand in his.

"This is the complete twenty-six-mile tour to the ocean in Paia," Philipo said.

But Lisa returned her gaze to the view from the window. She heard him breathe out as he relaxed. She almost smiled but ducked her head, trying to hide it.

"When we get to the Maui Mountain Riders Base, we will watch the sunrise. After we enjoy the sunrise, we will watch the Maui bike industry safety video and enjoy coffee, juice, and pastries."

Tom began to circle the back of Lisa's hand with his thumb. Lisa could feel her insides warm. Maybe she needed to remove her hand? She couldn't decide.

"After this stop, I will tell you more until the bike tour begins," the tour guide said.

It was difficult to enjoy the predawn view outside the van until they got to the summit. The view was mostly black and starting that daybreak gray. The van pulled up to the Mountain Bike Riders Summit just as it was beginning to turn amber. The group unloaded at a viewing area just for the sunrise. "It's spectacular!" Emma whispered excitedly, but mostly in wonder, which was unusual for Emma. The sunrise was so remarkable that the entire group was silently in awe at the spectacle. They stood there for several minutes.

As Tom reached for Lisa's hand, she became rigid, but she sighed and let their hands entwine. Tom eventually squeezed her hand softly, yet Lisa was no longer sure if he was manipulating her or if he was sincere. She had thought he was genuine before, but now, after his confession, she wondered if this was just a game to him.

After a while, when the pink sky began to lighten, Philipo said, "Let us go inside and watch the video."

The group trouped inside and watched a bike safety video and drank coffee and juice and ate pastries.

They boarded the van to Haleakala to hear about the history, geography, and rare plants and animals in Maui. Tom snagged Lisa's hand as soon as they sat down.

"This rare and sacred landscape vibrates with stories of ancient and modern Hawaiian culture. This protects the bond between the land and its people," Philipo started when the group returned to the van.

When she felt Tom caress the back of her hand, Lisa breathed in to relax. She couldn't help but close her eyes, enjoying its warmth.

"The park also cares for endangered species," Philipo continued. "Some of which exist nowhere else. Renew your spirit amid stark volcanic landscapes and sub-tropical rain forests with an unforgettable hike through the backcountry."

If she looked at him, she'd give in.

"Your tour of Haleakala National Park might include a glimpse of a native bird, breezes through the bamboo forest, or the sun on your back as you hike volcanic landscape."

Lisa opened her eyes and looked up at Tom. He smiled and, with his other hand, gently touched her face.

"Haleakala, or the East Maui Volcano, is a massive shield volcano that forms more than seventy-five percent of the Hawaiian Maui. The rest of the other twenty-five percent of the island is formed by another volcano, Mauna Kahalawai, also referred to as the West Maui Mountains."

She closed her eyes again and breathed in, feeling the sexual tension between them. She wanted to yield to these feelings so much.

"The tallest peak of Haleakala, meaning the House of the Sun, at ten thousand and twenty-three feet, is Puu Ulaula, meaning Red Hill."

She was afraid to give in. If she did, he would have more control over her.

"From the summit, you will look down into a massive depression some seven miles across and two miles wide and two thousand six hundred feet deep."

If Lisa gave in, Tom might never change and grow up. She knew he needed to.

"The surrounding walls are steep and the interior is mostly barren-looking with a scattering of volcano cones," Philipo said.

He slowly bent over and pulled her head closer and softly caressed her lips with his. She didn't pull away.

"Early Hawaiians applied the name Haleakala to the general mountain," Philipo said. "Haleakala is also the name of the peak on the southwestern edge of Kaupo Gap. In Hawaiian folklore, the depression, crater, at the summit of Haleakala, was the home of the grandmother of the demigod Maui. According to the legend, Maui's grandmother helped him capture the sun and force it to slow its journey across the sky to lengthen the day."

She paused. What was she doing? Wasn't she encouraging him?

"Contrary to popular belief, Haleakala is not volcanic in organ," Philipo said. "Nor can it accurately be called a caldera—which is formed when a summit collapses to form a depression."

Tom deepened the kiss. Lisa slightly tried to pull away. He gently tightened his hold on the back of her head. He eased her back toward him. He licked her bottom lip with his tongue.

"Scientists believe that Haleakala's crater was formed when the headwalls of two large erosional valleys merged at the summit of the volcano."

She succumbed and relaxed into the kiss. He swept his tongue in, and she moaned. Tom pulled back a little, and she followed him. Lisa felt him smile.

"These valleys formed the two large gaps," Philipo said. "Koolau on the north side and Kaupo on the south—on either side of the depression."

He tilted his head and deepened the kiss again. She knew she was in trouble. She was yielding to him again. *Oh, dear! What should she do?*

"Mcdonald, Abbot, and Peterson state it this way… Haleakala is far smaller than many volcanic craters, calderas."

Lisa put her hand on Tom's shoulder and somewhat pushed. He leaned back a little and locked eyes with her.

"There is an excellent chance that it is not extinct but only dormant."

They were both breathing raggedly and heavily. Tom swooped in and kissed Lisa powerfully. He tangled his fingers in her hair and pulled her close. She moaned.

"And strictly speaking, it is not of volcanic origin, beyond the fact that it is in a volcanic mountain."

She gently pulled away. "No," she whispered softly, shaking her head.

"No?" he whispered back, raising his eyebrows.

"Here we are, folks. The crater, the summit. You can take pictures, stretch a little bit and then you will put on your bicycle gear."

"No, Tom. Stop," Lisa gently pushed him away and stepped over his legs. He stood up behind her and pulled her close to him. She breathed in deeply and breathed out. Oh, she was so close to giving in. He heated her insides too much. Then she softly pushed his hands off her waist. He tightened instead and pulled her close, kissed her neck, and licked her ear. She shuddered. She was still affected by him. He tightened his hold on her even more and sighed. She was afraid he wouldn't let go, then he did. She got off the van.

Lisa walked over to Olive and stood close to her and Mason. Olive hugged her. They took some pictures as they played around and goofed off. Eventually, they were handed their Columbia sportswear windbreakers, gloves, helmets, and jackets. After donning their gear, they were expertly fitted and issued a state-of-the-art Volcano Chrome Cruiser Bike with heavy-duty breaks.

"You will begin your twenty-six-mile cruise down the slopes, which include the famous series of switchbacks and upcountry Kula," Philipo said.

Tom tried to jockey beside Lisa, but she shot him a scathing look. He backed off. "You will ride through Makawao town and sugarcane and pineapple fields on the lower slopes of Haleakala," Philipo said. "You will continue to cruise down to the Pacific Ocean where you will end at Paia beach park. We will stop for lunch at Makawao. You will have opportunities to stop for pictures at specific vistas and overlooks. The van will follow you along the way for safety and support. Any questions before you start, ladies and gentlemen?"

When no one answered, Philipo shouted, "And off you go!"

CHAPTER 31

Lisa took off like a shot as the bikers began heading down the hill. Tom stood up on his bike and began peddling harder to catch up with her.

"Hey, jackass."

Tom looked over at Bill. "What the hell, man?"

"Give her some space… *man*. Let her *miss* you," Bill said as they cruised down the hill at a comfortable speed rather than the breakneck haste Tom wanted to fly.

"I don't want her to miss me," Tom complained.

"If she misses you, she might want you back."

"Hmmm," Tom muttered. "You think?"

"Yes-s-s," Bill answered, a little testily. "Quit acting like you're in junior high or the next thing she'll be saying is that you're stalking her."

"Oh." Tom pouted. "But I don't want her to forget me."

"What does she say?"

"To wait six months."

"How old *are* you?" Bill asked.

"What?"

"You're not twelve. Six months is not that long these days. Get a grip. What happens after six months?"

"I don't know."

"What happens during the six months?" Bill asked.

"I'm supposed to grow up and figure out what I want in life and whether I really want her and really love her."

"Do you?" Bill asked.

"Do I what?" Tom scratched his head with one hand while the other guided the bike.

"Do you know what you really want in life? Do you really want kids running around, a picket fence, and a little white house? And a wedding ring?"

"I'm not sure… yet. I know I love her." Tom perked up.

"To girls like Lisa, when you say *love*, they think wedding rings."

"Oh." Tom ran his fingers through his hair.

"Take six months and figure it out."

"Oh." Tom blew out a breath and nodded slowly.

"It'll help you grow up. It'll help you figure out what you want. It'll help you figure out if you love her."

"But I do love her," Tom protested.

"Got one down and two more to go."

"Oh, yeah." Tom grimaced. "Come on, man. Give her some space. She's asked for it. She didn't slam the door in your face. She just stepped back from it."

"But what if she forgets about me in six months?"

"Then she's not your soulmate."

"Soulmate? Getting a little lovey-dovey and personal there?"

"Yeah, Sophia's been on me a little bit. We've been discussing your situation, like we know all there is to know and don't have our own issues to discuss because neither you nor Lisa is talking." Bill wiggled his eyebrows.

Tom laughed.

"That's the spirit!" Bill laughed too. "Perk up, dude. She won't forget you."

"How would you know?" Tom scoffed.

"Because I've seen the way she looks at you when she thinks you don't see. When she thinks no one else is looking. She's definitely in love with you. What were her words again?"

"Grow up and be certain of what I want," Tom said, pouting a little.

"Well then?"

"Okay. Okay," Tom laughed.

"Good. Now let me go catch up with the love of my life," Bill chuckled, taking off on his bike.

"All right already!" Tom hooted.

Bill rode off.

Tom had a lot of thinking to do. He really wanted Lisa. He really felt he loved her—a feeling he never had before. None of the girls he'd dated before ever gave him this feeling. Like he could never live without her. Like he could kiss her forever… without the sex. *Wow!* Like he could be with her forever… without the kissing. *Ooh.* That would never do. But he could—when in her company. *That's strange to me but almost satisfying.* He hated to admit it, but maybe Lisa and Bill spoke the truth. He had a lot of thinking to do. But six months? How fast—or slow—would that go?

He could see Lisa, her face turned to the ocean, the only pure thing in his life, and he suddenly wanted nothing more than to be worthy of her. To spend his life proving himself a good enough man to stand by her side. He had almost destroyed them both.

Now he needed to make it right.

Tom looked over the beautiful landscape and ocean in front of the bikers as they coasted down the hill. The sugarcane fields were blowing in the wind. The green stalks were waving their flower heads. He could see the turquoise water in the distance. This bike ride had been a good idea.

For the rest of the day, Tom stayed away from Lisa. During lunch in Makawao, he sat next to Bill, Noah, and Mason on the opposite end of the picnic table away from her. When he climbed onto the van that took them back to the hotel, he waited to see where she sat and then took a seat in a different row.

After packing, when everyone played in the pool back at the hotel, he kept his distance. He missed her, but if what Bill said had been true, then she needed some space. He didn't. He knew what he wanted—her. He wanted to spend nights curled up on the couch together. He wanted to wake up to see her beautiful face and blue eyes staring back at him. He wanted to feed her breakfast every morning and dinner at night. He wasn't sure about the wedding rings, picket fence, or kids though. He just wanted her—forever.

They boarded the airplane with assigned seats in first class. Everyone else paired up, so Tom ended up sitting by Lisa. He tried to not talk to her but couldn't resist holding her hand during the takeoffs and landings. She seemed shaky on those. He felt a little thrill when she thanked him, convinced she appreciated his presence. But while they cruised, he took out a magazine from the back of the seat in front of him and read it, giving her plenty of space but still fully aware of her presence beside him.

The group departed the plane in Houston. Alice, Jim, and Olive's father planned to pick them up. While the buddy mooners hadn't been couples when they left, they came back as couples. Except for Lisa and Tom.

Tom climbed into a cab by himself and headed back to his apartment wondering what Lisa would be doing the following day before having to return to work. It would have been so much more fun for the two of them to be hanging out together rather than unpacking, doing laundry, and watching late-night TV alone.

That afternoon, his younger brother, Elijah, dropped by.

"Hey, Tom." He smiled as Tom answered the door. "How did the vacation go? Meet any cute girls in Hawaii?"

"As a matter of fact, I did, but we fought at the end, and I'm not supposed to contact her for six months," Tom answered. His eyes dropped, and he ran his hand through his hair. "Six months?" Elijah asked. "What'd you do, bud?"

The men sat down on the couch in the living room. "You remember Maria? Olive's cousin?" Tom asked. "Sorry, do you want something to drink, by the way?"

"Nah," Elijah answered. "Continue. What happened?"

"Maria tried to cut in while I danced with Lisa, the girl I really like," Tom sighed.

"What? Women don't do that!" Elijah exclaimed.

"It's the twenty-first century," Tom said. "They're allowed to do that today, I suppose."

"Was she rude about it?".

"No," Tom huffed. "Seductive! In front of Lisa, the girl I'm pursuing."

"Wow!" Elijah said. "That's not helpful."

"Not only that, the wedding began the start of the vacation. In the end, Maria stayed in Maui to catch up with us before we left! Then she draped herself all over me as Lisa came out of the hotel. I tried to push her away politely, but it wasn't enough. She really laid it on thick, and Lisa got upset. Lisa said Maria would always be around and chasing me, and I had to deal with her," Tom said, frowning.

"What are you going to do? What can you do to prove your love to Lisa?" Elijah asked.

Tom moaned. "I guess I'm going to think about what she wants me to do. To think about forever and what that entails. If I can stay in a relationship for a long time," Tom sighed. "I'm sure I can. I don't like the dating around anymore or the one-night stands. I'm tired of the girls that don't want a long-term relationship. I'm tired of looking for someone like her when she's *it*. She's smart, intelligent, sweet, and has a great sense of humor. She's shy in public—mostly, but quite vocal in private. She's adorable," Tom sighed. "Elijah, I love her. I miss her already."

Tom proceeded to tell his brother all about Lisa and continued to tell him about the rest of the vacation—the buddy moon.

CHAPTER 32

*I*n the weeks following the buddy moon in Hawaii, Lisa slowly settled back into her life. Her luggage must have gotten lost again because it arrived a few days after she returned home. She now had double the clothes, hairbrush, and toiletries she needed. She put the extras aside for the future. Three weeks after coming home, she got the Bella Contract, which meant she was set financially for a while.

In addition to her professional work, she finally painted Tom's picture from the sketch she'd done in Hawaii. That took her a while to do. At first, she felt so mad at him that she couldn't look at the sketch without crying, then she couldn't look at it without being angry. But when she finished, she admired how strong he looked. It wasn't just his physique, she had captured the joy in his face and his unselfish nature.

When she looked at the finished product, the whole trip came rushing back but in a good way.

While painting a customer one day, Olive's cousin, Maria, stopped by with someone she introduced as Kirk. Lisa glanced in her direction and quickly refocused on the striking features of her customer, not wanting to interrupt her concentration. It had taken a long time to paint this particular customer. She had outstanding black hair with blue highlights and wore a beautiful red dress that complimented her skin tone. She was a delight to paint, and she would be paying Lisa very well.

"I'm sorry," Maria said.

Lisa continued drawing her client. "For what?"

"For trying to sabotage you."

Lisa looked up at Maria. "Well, you won. Are you happy now?"

Even though Lisa and Tom weren't together at the moment, Lisa still decided to give Maria grief.

Maria looked at Kirk sheepishly.

Kirk nodded toward Lisa. "Go on," he said. "Finish it."

Maria closed her eyes and looked chagrinned. "I've promised to try to be nicer to people from now on," Maria said.

"Good luck," Lisa answered. She really wanted to add a "with that" snarky comment but felt like Maria actually looked contrite. She let it pass.

Lisa did okay now, but she missed Tom. She had cried a ton of tears over him and finally stopped and refused to cry anymore. She felt Tom was the love of her life. He was supposed to show up after six months, and it had been six months—to the day—today. Now, Lisa felt sorry for herself. She had not wanted to turn Tom away that day in Hawaii. Deep in her heart though, she felt like if she didn't force the distance, he would never change. He had to want to change his lifestyle, and he had to have the space to figure out that he wanted to make that change. She felt sad and lonely. All this work and no Tom. Together, they would be perfect, but he wasn't here. Her heart didn't feel free or joyful. It felt closed off.

As she sat there thinking about everything she had lost, her phone rang.

"Tom?" She couldn't believe her ears.

"Lisa," Tom said.

"Yes, Tom?"

"It's been six months," he stated.

"It has," she answered.

"Uh… c-can I come over and talk with you? Today?" Tom stuttered.

"Right now?"

"Yes," he said.

"I have a client coming in the afternoon," Lisa answered. "But now is a good time. Yes, you can."

"I'll be there shortly," Tom said.

He's coming over! Lisa was ecstatic. She tittered about the house, cleaning here and straightening there. She made earl grey tea in her favorite teapot. She couldn't wait until he got here.

She heard a knock on her door. She almost skipped answering, looking forward to a big hug from Tom. She opened the door with a flourish.

"To…" she said, but she froze. There stood Grey, her old boyfriend. The one who had raped her. He looked as handsome as ever in his beautiful, collared light-violet shirt and blue jeans. And yet, his good looks were smudged with evil from her memories with him.

"What do you want?" she snapped.

"Now, is that any way to greet an old friend?" Grey schmoozed, stepping into her house.

"You're not an old friend. You're the one who raped me!" Lisa almost shouted.

"Now you know that wasn't rape," he sneered. "That was consensual sex."

"Get off my property!" Lisa snapped again.

"Not till I tell you what I want."

"What?" Lisa asked angrily.

"Can I come in for this conversation?" Grey took another step inside her door. "And sit down on the couch, for old time's sake?"

"No! What are you doing here, Grey?" she demanded.

"I've been thinking that we should get back together again. Like before."

She shook her head, wondering why he was suddenly interested in her again.

"You know I always care about you, darlin'."

In a flash, it hit her. It was her money. He must have heard that she was finally secure.

"You must be out of your mind!" she shouted. "I would never take you back. You embarrassed me. You raped me, and now, I'm pretty sure you want to take my money too?"

"Now, darlin' …" Grey smirked, reaching for her.

"Go away!" Lisa shouted and began to close the door in his face. Instead, Grey stepped inside and into her space. He kicked the door closed and pushed her up against the wall. He tried to kiss her, but she saw it coming and turned her head, making him kiss her cheek instead. She tried to knee him in the groin, but he moved his knee in time to block her, then he grabbed her head and held it still as he kissed her right on the mouth. Lisa almost gagged. She was so furious and scared. He was going to do it again. She had no recourse other than to fight, and this time, she would.

"Get out of here!"

Just then, her door opened again.

Thank God Grey hadn't locked it, she thought, ready to scream *help* to whoever it was.

Tom stood there, scowling. He grabbed Grey around the throat with his arm, squeezing until Grey let go of Lisa. Grey released Lisa's hands and clawed at Tom's arms to breathe, but Tom refused to free him. Grey eventually passed out. Tom let him slide to the floor.

"Thank you!" Lisa breathed. She threw her arms around Tom's neck. "Oh, Tom! I'm so glad you're here!"

Tom brushed back her hair from her face. He gently rubbed down her face to her neck with his finger.

"Oh, baby," he sighed. He put his hand behind her neck, leaned down, and kissed her gently. The kiss soon turned into a scorching one. Lisa didn't want to let go, but eventually, Tom raised his head. "I was so shocked when I opened the door. I thought you had moved on. That he was a new boyfriend, then I realized what it was."

"No. He just showed up—"

He pulled her close. "I know. I realized that. And then I became so angry. I couldn't let that stranger hurt you."

"He's not a stranger," Lisa sobbed. "He's Grey. The one who raped me. He was going to do it again. I think he wants my money."

"Lisa, I don't care if you have money or not. I love you for you and want you in my life," Tom cried.

"Oh, Tom," Lisa said. Suddenly, she remembered she had wanted him to change. "Have you changed?"

"Lisa, I want you to know that I love you. I haven't been with anyone else since the vacation."

"You haven't?"

"No, sweetheart. I've thought long and hard about your request. I love you. I *can* be with only one person. I *can* be faithful to one person—if that person is you, dear."

"Oh, sweet Tom," Lisa breathed. "I love you too."

"First let me take out the trash," he said, looking at Grey who was moaning and just waking up. "Hey, man," Tom said to Grey. "It's time to go outside." He picked Grey up by the collar and started to push him outside.

The doorbell rang.

Tom and Lisa looked at each other. Tom reached over and opened the door. Lisa stayed behind him.

Outside, on the doorstep, was an elderly man with gray hair.

Lisa stepped around Tom and said, "Mr. Green, can I help you?"

"You looked like you needed help. I called the sheriff," Mr. Green said.

"You did?" Lisa asked.

"And you are?" Tom asked.

"I'm her neighbor," Mr. Green said. "I live across the street. I caught the whole thing on my doorbell camera."

Just then, a sheriff's car drove up. When the sheriff and Deputy Wells walked up, Grey stood up.

"This man attacked me," Grey said, pointing at Tom.

Lisa started to yell, "Oh no you don't! You attacked me, and Tom rescued me. Mr. Green caught it all on his doorbell camera!"

Grey turned pale.

"Wait!" Sheriff Thompson said.

Everyone got quiet.

"You!" Pointing to Grey, Sheriff Thompson said, "I will take your statement. Deputy Wells will take yours," he said, pointing to Tom. "Then we'll get yours." Pointing to Lisa and Mr. Green.

Tom went with the male officer and told his side of the story, then Sheriff Thompson talked to Mr. Green, and Deputy Carol Wells talked to Lisa. Grey had permission to leave.

"Now I'm not really sure how to get the film off the phone," Mr. Green to Deputy Wells said. "But if you'll come help me, it'll prove what the three of us are saying is right."

Lisa told Deputy Wells what happened and got up the nerve to press charges against Grey. She also decided to file a restraining order against him.

When the sheriff, deputy, and Mr. Green left, Tom and Lisa went back inside.

"Let's celebrate," Lisa said, getting a bottle of wine and handing him a glass.

"To us." Tom winked, indicating for her to pick up her glass, now full of wine.

Her head bobbed as she slowly forced air into her lungs.

"To us." Lisa took a sip. "Tom?" She put down her glass of wine and began twisting her hands.

"Yeah?" He sat down his glass on the table and waited for her to continue.

"Is there an us?" She stumbled on her words. "I mean, what exactly are we doing?"

His eyes flashed for a brief second, and he sucked in a breath. "Do you want there to be?" He crossed his arms over his chest and spread his legs. "What happens to us depends on what you want to do."

Lisa's mouth dropped open. "Uh…" she started and then hung her head, feeling overwhelmed.

Tom squeezed his eyes shut and took a deep breath. He uncrossed his arms and dropped them by his side. "I love you, Lisa. I want to be with you. I will be there for you. I will be a one-woman man. You make me want to be that. Forever."

Lisa inhaled deeply, her eyes wide. She wasn't expecting that. He said he loved her… but to want her forever? Was she getting ahead of herself? She felt like smiling but was not sure. Yet.

Tom's voice was hoarse. He took a step toward her. "Lisa, I want you. I will wait for you. However long it takes. I won't push you or crowd you. I did in the beginning. Yes. And it worked. But I won't do it again!"

"Have you changed, Tom?" Lisa asked.

"Well, yes, I've been traveling."

"Traveling?" she asked.

"Yes. Actually, at first, I couldn't leave the country without you, but I finally went to Kenya. I tried running away. I tried to pick up a woman but backed off when I looked into her eyes and they weren't your exciting blue ones," Tom confessed. "All I could think about was you and how you wanted me to change."

"*How* have you changed, Tom?"

"I haven't been with anyone else since you," he explained. "I tried to go on a date with another woman. I decided you were done with me and I would move on, but as soon as I started talking to her, I thought about you and how intelligent you are. I apologized and left," he said and hung his head.

"Should I believe you this time too?" she asked sarcastically.

Tom lifted his head. "It's true." Then bowed it again and sighed. "I was hardly breathing without you, but believe what you want," he said sadly. "Maybe I should go. You don't want to believe me." He turned to go.

Lisa realized he might leave, and she didn't want him to go. "Tom…" she said hesitantly.

Then he turned back, beseeching her. "Lisa, I've tried really hard to forget you. I've tried to go back to my old life, but I couldn't forget about you or our two weeks together. I couldn't forget your lovely sky-blue eyes or your beautiful golden blonde hair." He stepped forward, closer, crowding her space. He reached out to push a strand of hair behind her ear and stroked it softly.

Lisa stood perfectly still and looked up into his baby-blue eyes.

"Lisa, I love your soft, soft lips," he said as he stroked her bottom lip with his thumb, then he put his hand on the back of her neck. "I don't want to date around. All I want is a life with you. I want to get engaged. Get married."

She gasped at his words and put her trembling hand to her mouth.

"I've told you how I feel. That hasn't changed." Tom's lips went into a straight line. "Sweetheart." He locked eyes with Lisa. "I'll wait until you're ready, but I need to know what you want."

Lisa felt her throat tighten with tears. *Was he really this sweet?* she paused, thinking.

"Do you mean that? Will you wait for me to decide if there is an 'us' or not?" she finally asked.

"Yes, Lisa." Tom looked very carefully at her expression. "Don't you believe me?"

"Of course, I do!" she answered hurriedly.

"Then, do you know what you want now?" Tom asked.

Lisa noticed he looked concerned.

He frowned, and his lips flattened out.

Lisa dropped her eyes, then she looked up and smiled. "I want an 'us.' I want a forever."

Tom grabbed her and spun her around. "Sweetheart!" He spun her again.

"Tom!" she laughed. His joy was infectious.

"How long?' he cried. "How long do we wait?"

"Can we start with dating?' Lisa asked, giggling.

"Dating?" Tom asked, looking confused, then brightened. "Yes! Dating! Where do you want to go?" he asked excitedly.

"Tom, don't you want to ask me out?" Lisa asked, smiling.

"Yes," he said, chuckling. "Want to get pizza? That can be our first date!"

"Now?"

"It's almost lunchtime!"

"Wait, Tom," Lisa said, holding up her hand. "I do have a client coming, but lunchtime can be squeezed in."

"What else?" Tom asked. Lisa noticed she trembled.

"What does forever look like? What does it mean to us?" she asked, still feeling lost. Tom smiled. He pulled something from his pocket. He dropped to one knee and showed her a velvet ring box. "Lisa, make me the happiest and luckiest man in the world and marry me!" He opened the ring box. "Lisa, will you marry me? That's what forever means… to me," Tom breathed excitedly. "I love you, Lisa. I think you are the most amazing person I've ever met. You are kind and helpful. You are intelligent and beautiful. I really do love you, sweetheart…" Tom paused. "You have my heart! I want to spend the rest of my life with you and telling our grandkids about how we met and the attraction was so instantaneous, that I knew you would be mine forever. Will you marry me?"

Was she willing to forgive him? He had such a past. He had lied to her by omission. Would he do it again? Did she know either way? Could she trust him now? Was he worth it? Was she willing to let go of the past and step into the future? With him? With marriage?

The answer was a resounding *yes!*

Lisa gasped, putting her hand to her mouth.

"Y-y-yes!" Lisa stumbled on her words. "Yes! Of course, I will!" she shouted.

Tom stood up, took out the ring, and gently placed the two-carat pear infinity twist diamond engagement ring on the third finger of her left hand.

Lisa brought the ring up and looked at it. She took a deep breath and smiled. It was a lot to take in. "Oh, Tom!"

He grabbed her around her waist and spun her around.

Lisa threw her head back and laughed with joy.

Her heart opened and she finally felt free.

THE END